Terrorism and Medical Responses

U.S. Lessons and Policy Implications

Yonah Alexander
and
Stephen D. Prior
Editors

Transnational Publishers, Inc.

Published and distributed by Transnational Publishers, Inc.
410 Saw Mill River Road
Ardsley, NY 10502, USA

Phone: 914-693-5100
Fax: 914-693-4430
E-mail: info@transnationalpubs.com
Web: www.transnationalpubs.com

Library of Congress Cataloging-in-Publication Data

[On File]

Manufactured in the United States of America

Contents

Part III: Selected Documents

About the Editors

Yonah Alexander

A former director of the Terrorism Studies Program at The George Washington University, Prof. Alexander is currently Director, Inter-University Center for Terrorism Studies (affiliated with academic institutions around the world). In addition, he is a Senior Fellow of the Potomac Institute for Policy Studies and Director of the International Center for Terrorism Studies, Potomac Institute for Policy Studies.

Educated at Columbia University, the University of Chicago, and the University of Toronto, Professor Alexander taught at The George Washington University; The American University; the Columbus School of Law at The Catholic University of America; Tel Aviv University; The City University of New York; and the State University of New York.

His research experience includes such appointments as Research Professor of International Affairs, The George Washington University; Senior Fellow, The Institute for Advanced Studies in Justice, School of Law, The American University; Research Associate, School of Journalism, Columbia University; Senior Staff Member, Center for Strategic and International Studies, Georgetown University; Director, Institute for Studies in International Terrorism, State University of New York; and Fellow, Institute of Social Behavior Pathology, the University of Chicago.

Dr. Alexander is Founding Editor of the International Journal on Minority and Group Rights. He also founded and edited *Terrorism: An International Journal* and *Political Communication and Persuasion: An International Journal*. He has published over eighty books on the subjects of international affairs, terrorism, and psychological warfare.

Stephen D. Prior

Dr. Prior trained as a life scientist with qualifications in microbiology and biochemistry. His research interests focused on microbial physiology resulting in over 20 years research experience in a wide range of multinational and biotechnological environments. He has been the Project Manager for US

Department of Defense contracts that exceed $500 million and has experience in management of large, multi-disciplinary teams operating in international collaborative efforts.

Dr. Prior is an acknowledged leader in the field of medical defense against the threat posed by biological weapons (BW) who, since 1986, has advised and worked closely with government and commercial defense staffs, world-wide, to develop integrated strategies of medical countermeasures for BW defense. He has wide experience over the past two decades in the defense industry, including appointments with the UK Ministry of Defense and NATO, as well as presenting scientific papers to the most important international meetings on BW defense. He has a unique knowledge of the issues relating to the threat posed by biological weapons, the role of medical countermeasures in countering the threat and the requirements to implement an effective strategy for defense in the military and civilian population.

Dr. Prior was the founding Research Director of the National Security Health Policy Center (NSHPC), based at the Potomac Institute for Policy Studies in Arlington, VA. The NSHPC serves to focus the debate on how existing and new or proposed legislation, policies, and procedures impact the ability of the United States government to maintain national security while preventing, detecting, and responding to a growing number of existing and emerging health threats including bioterrorism.

Preface

Terrorism—the calculated employment of violence, or the threat of violence by individuals, subnational groups, and state actors to attain political, social, and economic objectives in the violation of law, intended to create an overwhelming fear in a target area larger than the victims attacked or threatened—is as old as civilization itself. Yet unlike their historical counterparts, present-day terrorists have introduced into contemporary life a new scale of violence in terms of conventional and unconventional threats and impact. The internationalization and brutalization of modern terrorism make it clear that we have entered into an Age of Super and Cyber Terrorism with its serious implications to national, regional, and global security concerns. Perhaps the most significant dangers are those relating to: the safety, welfare, and rights of ordinary people; the stability of the state system; the health of economic development; the expansion of democracy; and perhaps even the survival of civilization itself.

These challenges became no longer a mere "threat assessment" on September 11, 2001. The brutal attacks on the United States, unprecedented in scope and sophistication, killing an estimated 6,000 people and wounding many others, represented the deadliest terrorist operations in world history. Nineteen terrorists hijacked four U.S. airliners, which they used to crash into the Twin Towers of the World Trade Center in New York; the Pentagon in Arlington, Virginia; and a third location, not the intended target, a field in Shanksville, Pennsylvania. At 8:45 a.m., American Airlines Flight 11, en route from Boston to Los Angeles with 81 passengers and 11 crew members, crashed into the North Tower of the World Trade Center. United Airlines Flight 175, also headed from Boston to Los Angeles and carrying 56 passengers and 9 crew members, slammed into the South Tower of the World Trade Center at 9:03 a.m. Twenty-five minutes later, American Airlines Flight 77, scheduled to fly from Washington Dulles International Airport to Los Angeles with 58 passengers and 6 crew members, crashed into the northwest side of the Pentagon. At 10:00 a.m., United Airlines Flight 93, headed from Newark to San Francisco and carrying 38 passengers and 7 crew members, crashed during a struggle between the hijackers and passengers in Pennsylvania.

These simultaneous and massive assaults aimed at America's most visible symbols of engineering prowess as well as an unmatched economic and military reputation, were linked to Usama bin Laden's al-Qaida.[1] The United States has

---

[1]   See Yonah Alexander and Michael S. Swetnam, eds., *Usama bin Laden's al-Qaida: Profile of a Terrorist Network* (Ardsley, N.Y.: Transnational Publishers, Inc., 2001).

declared a war against al-Qaida as well as against international terrorism in general. As this book goes into press, Anthrax has been found in letters addressed to NBC News in New York City and the office of the Senate majority leader, Tom Daschle. Although there is not credible information to confirm that these incidents, as well as other similar cases across the United States, are linked to bin Laden's network, the fact is that his group has made numerous efforts to obtain weapons of mass destruction, including biological, chemical, and nuclear capability.[2] In fact, al-Qaida's calling for a Jihad (Holy War) against the United States and its allies justifies the utilization of as much force as possible to attack the "enemies of God."

It is becoming increasingly clear that the medical response to the challenges of terrorism is now even more critical than ever before. Some thirty years ago, the perspectives on emergency medical preparedness could be summed up as follows:

(1) The public has changed its attitude and rejects decision makers' passivity when a citizen's life and limb are threatened by terrorism and by other disasters.

(2) There is a common, uncomplicated model of human injury as the result of terrorism weaponry.

(3) There is a common physiological response to terrorist injury.

(4) There is a simple, common model of resuscitation, which should be initiated on-site.

(5) Twenty percent or more of the lives now lost in terrorist attacks or other disasters could be saved and untold crippling could be prevented.

(6) There is a need for national emergency medical systems.

(7) Medical rescue is an essential part of counterterrorism.[3]

In light of the tragic and diabolical events of September 11, 2001, that claimed the lives of so many innocent citizens of the United States, there is a need to examine these observations in order to provide an updated framework for medical response to current and future terrorist threats.

The introductory section of the volume was prepared after the events of September 11, 2001. All the other papers in the volume were prepared

---

[2]   See Yonah Alexander and Milton Hoenig, eds., *Super Terrorism: Biological, Chemical, Nuclear* (Ardsley, N.Y.: Transnational Publishers, Inc., 2001).

[3]   Martin Elliot Silverstein, M.D., "Emergency Medical Preparedness," in Yonah Alexander, ed., *Terrorisn: An International Journal*, Vol. 1, No. 1 (1977), p. 62.

following the March 2001 seminar on "Terrorism and Medical Responses: U.S. Lessons and Policy Implications," which was cosponsored by the National Security Health Policy Center and the International Center for Terrorism Studies of the Potomac Institute for Policy Studies in cooperation with the Inter-University Center for Terrorism Studies. It was determined by the editors that these papers should be included as originally written in order that they reflect the work presented at the seminar. As such, they represent a record of the status of academic concerns within the medical community about possible terrorist incidents prior to the events of September 11, 2001. The focus at the time of the seminar was the threat to U.S. citizens at home and abroad. It is clear on re-reading the papers that many of the concerns raised at the time of the seminar were realized in the attacks on the World Trade Center and the Pentagon and that many of the concerns still remain. There is much that needs to be done to mitigate or remove the threat posed by terrorist actions, and it is clear that the medical community will play a critical role in an effective response. This volume is published in an effort to catalyze the thinking in the medical community by those who will rely on its capabilities in the future.

The opinions and comments in this volume are those of the editors and the authors and do not necessarily represent the position of the Potomac Institute for Policy Studies in this important area of public concern. It is anticipated that some of the comments will be further explored in forthcoming work that the National Security Health Policy Center and the International Center for Terrorism Studies will undertake.

In the interim, the editors of this volume felt that four topics merited special attention and commissioned specific articles to reflect those topics. In the first article, Professor Yonah Alexander explores the terrorist threat and the likely future actions of some of the most active of the current terrorist groups. In the second article, Dr. Betram Brown and Dr. Stephen Prior discuss the threat from biotrerrorism and the current vulnerability of the United States, and the need to strengthen the country's response capability through the public health service. The third article by Dr. George Everly examines the psychological aspects of responding to mass terrorist attacks. The final article by Dr. Prior reviews the probability of a bioterrorist attack occurring in the United States. The authors of these articles have been actively working in the field of terrorism for many decades and offer insights that are valuable given the rude awakening that the nation had on September 11, 2001.

We wish to thank Michael S. Swetnam, CEO and Chairman of the Board, Potomac Institute for Policy Studies, for his continuing encouragement and support. We also wish to thank Dr. Ronald Blanck, President of the University of North Texas—Health Science Center, for his financial support of the National Security Health Policy Center and his personal support for the studies discussed in this volume. Important contributions were made by a research team coordinated by James T. Kirkhope of the International Center for Terrorism Studies, and comprised of: Adam Barrer, Melissa Brewster, John Evans, Kim Fadden, Meredith Gilchrest, Bryan Koontz, Jr., Alon Lanir, Peter H. Leddy, Kerrie Martin, Vivek Narayanan, Manuel Pabon, Veris Prasarntree, Jay Rosen, Chris Rush, Joseph Stephenson, Linda Truong, and Christopher Wallace.

Prof. Yonah Alexander
Senior Fellow and Director
International Center for Terrorism Studies
Potomac Institute for Policy Studies

Dr. Stephen D. Prior
Research Director
National Security Health Policy Center
Potomac Institute for Policy Studies

October 15, 2001

Part I

The New World Order:
Post-September 11, 2001, Lessons

Introduction

In the wake of the appalling events of September 11, 2001, the editors of this volume felt that three topics merited special attention and commissioned specific articles to reflect those topics. In the first article Professor Yonah Alexander explores the terrorist threat and the likely future actions of some of the most active of the current terrorist groups. In the second article Dr Bertram Brown and Dr Stephen Prior explore the threat from bioterrorism and the current vulnerability of the United States, and the need to strengthen the country's response capability through the public health service. The third article by Dr George Everly discusses the psychological aspects of responding to mass terrorist attacks. The final article by Dr Prior reviews the probability of a bioterrorist attack occurring in the U.S. The authors of these articles have been actively working in the field of terrorism for many decades and offer insights that are valuable given the rude awakening that the nation had on terrorism "Day of Infamy."

Terrorism in the Twenty-First Century: An Overview

Yonah Alexander

I.   Introduction: A Definitional Focus[1]

Many governments have failed to appreciate the extent and implications of the terrorist threat to modern societies. As a result, a large number of countries, including Western democracies, have not developed strong commitments to deal effectively with the challenge. A major reason for this failure is the definitional and moral confusion over what constitutes terrorism. Every sovereign state reserves to itself the political and legal authority to define terrorism in the context of domestic and foreign affairs. And yet, some governments speak with a bewildering variety of voices on the subject of terrorism.

An analysis of various governmental and intergovernmental as well as academic views on the subject, indicates that there is no consensus of what terrorism is. Nevertheless, there seems to be an agreement related to several components, such as the nature of the act (e.g. unlawful); perpetrators (e.g. individuals, groups, states); objectives (e.g. political); intended outcomes and motivations (e.g. fear and frustration); targets (e.g. victims); and methods (e.g. hijacking).

On the basis of these elements, is it reasonable to adopt the following working definition for the purpose of this article: terrorism is defined as the calculated employment or the threat of violence by individuals, subnational groups, and state actors to attain political, social, and economic objectives in the violation of law, intended to create an overwhelming fear in a target area larger than the victims attacked or threatened.

---

[1]   For more details see Yonah Alexander and Edgar H. Brenner, editors, *Terrorism and the Law*, (Ardsley, N.Y.: Transnational Publishers, Inc., 2001).

II.   Future Prospects: Twenty-First Century Trends[2]

A.   *Reasons for Future Terrorism Growth*

The bloody record of terror violence, particularly as demonstrated dramatically on September 11, 2001, underscores, once again, that terrorism is a permanent fixture of international life, epitomizing the state of anarchy of modern societies which is increasingly becoming a universal nightmare. It is safe to assume, therefore, that terrorism will continue into the twenty-first century. This prognosis is borne from the reality that many of the causes that motivate terrorists, such as ideological, theological, political and national animosities, will remain unresolved, thereby encouraging terrorists to instigate violence to achieve political, economic and social change.

What is of particular concern is the fact that countries like Afghanistan, Iraq, and the Sudan have provided the most dangerous international terrorist network in existence, al-Qaida and its leader Osama bin Laden safe-haven and other assistance for organizational, training, and operational purposes. Bin Laden's goals are to overthrow corrupt Western-oriented governments in predominantly Muslim countries. To achieve these goals bin Laden maintains formal and informal relationships with like-minded Sunni Islamic terrorist groups in some 60 countries throughout the world, including Algeria, Bosnia, Canada, Chechnya, Egypt, Eritrea, France, Libya, Pakistan, Philippines, Saudi Arabia, Somalia, United Kingdom, United States, and Yemen.

The activities of al-Qaida and its affiliate organizations have long been financed with bin Laden's personal fortune estimated at $300 million. In addition, the group and many other affiliate militant Islamic-oriented bodies have been funded by external sources, using charitable structures as fronts.

Perceiving the United States as a prime target, bin Laden's operative had been engaged in various complex operations such as the bombing of the World Trade Center in New York City in 1993; the 1996 attack at the Khobar Towers in Saudi Arabia; and bombings of the U.S. Embassies in Kenya and Tanzania in 1998; the attack on the USS Cole in Aden in 2000; and the latest brutal assaults in New York City, Washington, D.C., and over Pennsylvania. While the preferred tactics of these operations have been vehicle bombs and multiple

---

2   See several recent studies such as: Yonah Alexander and Donald Musch, eds., *Terrorism: Documents of Local and International Control - U.S Perspectives, Vol. 26* (Dobbs Ferry, New York: Oceana Publications, 2001); Yonah Alexander, Herbert M. Levine, and Michael S. Swetnam, eds., *ETA: Profile of a Terrorist Group* (Ardsley, New York: Transnational Publishers, 2001); and Yonah Alexander and Michael S. Swetnam, eds., *Usama bin Laden's al-Qaida: Profile of a Terrorist Network* (Ardsley, New York: Transnational Publishers, 2001).

hijackings, it is suspected that bin Laden is actively seeking weapons of mass destruction (biological, chemical, and nuclear).

These "super" weapons are slowly emerging upon the terrorist scene. That is, as technological developments offer new capabilities for terrorist groups, the modus operandi of terrorist groups may subsequently alter. According to various intelligence reports at least a dozen terrorist groups, in addition to the bin Laden network, have shown an interest in acquiring or actively attempting to obtain biological, chemical, or nuclear weapons. Clearly, the Aum Shinrikyo Japanese terrorist doomsday cult, mounting the Sarin gas attack on the Tokyo subway in 1995 which killed 12 people and injured over five thousand, was seeking more lethal weapons when its leaders were arrested.

And yet, having achieved considerable tactical success during the past three decades, terrorists sometimes find it politically expedient to restrain the level of political violence. In light of the Sepember 2001 attacks, it is important to understand that these self-imposed restraints will not persist indefinitely, and future incidents may continue to be costly in terms of human lives and property. Certain conditions, such as religious extremism or perceptions that the "cause" is lost, could provide terrorists with an incentive to escalate their attacks dramatically.

In sum, there are several specific reasons why terrorism will grow in the future. First, terrorism has proved very successful in attracting publicity, disrupting the activities of government and business, and causing significant death and destruction. Second, arms, explosives, supplies, financing, and secret communications are readily available. Third, an international support network of groups and states exists which greatly facilitates the undertaking of terrorist activities.

B.   *Biological, Chemical and Nuclear Threats*[3]

It is conceivable that a highly motivated and desperate terrorist group with technological and financial assets will attempt to improve its bargaining leverage by resorting to mass destruction violence. Such a determined group would be willing to take numerous risks in acquiring and using such weapons. Because the confrontation is seen by many groups as an "all-or-nothing" struggle, in case of failure the terrorists are prepared to bring the government to submission, actually to use these weapons and in the process to bring devastation and destruction to many lives including their own. Surely for these terrorists, the fear of deterrence or retaliation does not exist as it does in the case of states.

---

[3]   See, for example, Yonah Alexander and Milton Hoenig, eds., *Super Terrorism: Biological, Chemical, Nuclear* (Ardsley, New York: Transnational Publishers, 2001).

It is obvious that the prospects of success for such a group would be enhanced if it had previously demonstrated high technological capabilities and a strong willingness to incur high risks involved in similar ventures. Even if there were some skepticism about the credibility of the threat, no rational government would lightly risk an unconventional incident. The danger here is that if one sub-national body succeeds in achieving its goals, then the temptation for other terrorist groups to use, or threaten to use, similar weapons may become irresistible.

In view of these considerations, the arsenal of tomorrow's terrorist might include biological, chemical, and nuclear instruments of massive death and destruction potential. These weapons are capable of producing from several thousand to several million casualties in a single incident, and of causing governmental disruption of major proportions and widespread public panic. In the aftermath of the September 11, 2001 attacks, we have already had a number of mass destruction related incidents. The United States admitted for the first time that the series of anthrax attacks across America could be the work of terrorists.

In sum, biological and chemical weapons have many advantages for terrorists. These benefits include their low cost, and the ease and speed of their production; further, they can be developed by individuals with a limited education and facilities. Weapon development requires only a minimum amount of tools and space, and equipment can be improvised or purchased often without arousing suspicion.

Notwithstanding the assumption that in the short term future biological and chemical terrorism is feasible technologically, the specter of nuclear terrorism such as the explosion of a nuclear bomb, the use of fissionable material as a radioactive poison, and the seizure and sabotage of nuclear facilities, is seen by many experts as plausible and by others as inevitable. At this time, however, a credible threat or hoax involving a nuclear device, holding for political or economic blackmail a reactor or other nuclear facility or shipment of reactor fuel or waste, and truck-bombing of a reactor, may be the most likely form of nuclear terrorism.

The attempts of bin Laden's network to obtain enriched uranium for the purpose of developing nuclear weapons is only the latest example of the potential threat. In late May 1998, bin Laden issued a statement entitled "The Nuclear Bomb of Islam" in which he stated that it is the duty of Muslims to prepare as much force as possible to attack the enemies of God.

It is likely that changing political, economic, and social patterns in the domestic and international situations which will occur in the foreseeable future might give rise to pressures and tensions that could motivate other terrorists to seek nuclear capabilities.

C.   Cyber Terrorism[4]

An emerging trend of international life is the growing threat of information warfare and cyber terrorism. "Information Warfare," as reflected in the manifold definitions offered as well as the coverage of the media, consists of a broad spectrum of threats ranging from electronic jamming to psychological operations underscoring the perpetrators' deliberate exploitation of military and civilian information systems' inherent vulnerabilities and thereby adversely affecting national and global security.

What is of particular concern is the prevailing assessment of intelligence agencies, strategic thinkers, and scientists that not only "hackers" and "crackers" (criminal "hackers") but also terrorists (individuals, groups, and state sponsors) are likely to intensify the exploitation of the new "equalizer" weapon as a form of "electronic warfare." It is estimated, for instance, that hostile low-risk perpetrators launching a well-coordinated attack with about thirty computer experts strategically placed around the globe and with a budget of approximately ten million dollars, could bring the United States, the only superpower, to its knees.

Clearly, there are numerous other devastating scenarios, including altering formulas for medication at pharmaceutical plants, "crashing" telephone systems, misrouting passenger trains, changing pressure in gas pipelines to cause valve failure, disrupting operations of air traffic control, triggering oil refinery explosions and fires, scrambling the software used by emergency services, "turning off" power grids, and detonating simultaneously hundreds of computerized bombs around the world.

In sum, this new medium of communication, command and control, supplemented by unlimited paralyzing and destructive keyboard attacks on civilian and military critical infrastructure nerve centers, forces us to think about the "unthinkable" with grave concern.

III.   Conclusions: Implications for Policy

Until September 11, 2001, many governments and people have failed to appreciate the magnitude and implications of the terrorist threat. Some countries tended to regard terrorism as a minor nuisance or irritant. As a result, a large number of countries have not developed a strong commitment to deal effectively with the problem of terrorism.

---

4   See, for instance, Yonah Alexander and Michael S. Swetnam, eds., *Cyber Terrorism and Information Warfare: Threats and Responses* (Ardsley, New York: Transnational Publishers, 2001); and Yonah Alexander and Milton Hoenig, eds., *Information Warfare and Cyber Terrorism: Threats and Responses, Vols. 1-4* (Dobbs Ferry, New York: Oceana Publications, 1999).

In the post September 11, 2001, period, there are several policy implications to be considered:

First, there are no simplistic or complete solutions to the dangers of terrorism. As the tactics utilized to challenge the authority of the state are and continue to be novel, so too must be the response by the instruments of the state. We must also be cautious to avoid the kinds of overreaction that could lead to repression and the ultimate weakening of the democratic institutions that we seek to protect.

Second, having achieved considerable tactical success during the past four decades, terrorists sometimes find it politically expedient to restrain the level of political violence. These self-imposed restraints will not persist indefinitely, and future incidents may continue to be costly in terms of human lives and property. Certain conditions, such as religious extremism or perceptions that the 'cause' is lost, could provide terrorists with an incentive to escalate their attacks dramatically.

Third, the vulnerability of modern society and its infrastructure, coupled with the opportunities for the utilization of sophisticated high-leverage conventional and unconventional weaponry, requires states both unilaterally, and in concert, to develop credible responses and capabilities to minimize future threats.

And fourth, national and international emergency medical systems must be established immediately. The logistics of an integrated system, the management of its information and resource allocation networks and communication links with intelligence agencies, law enforcement, and first responders require continuing strategic planning, research, and development.

The Rise of the Fourth Horseman?

Bertram Brown, M.D., and Stephen Prior

To him was given the power over a quarter of the earth, with the right to kill by sword and famine, by pestilence and wild beasts.

Revelations 6:8.

Executive Summary

Bioterrorism serves as both a unique and special threat and a focus for dealing with the 21st Century problem of mass destruction and escalating threats from terrorist acts. The potential of mass terrorism using biological agents, or the threat from emerging diseases, highlights our need to strengthen the public health institutions of the United States and other countries. Successful implementation of measures that deal with biological issues will also serve to strengthen our ability to deal with the threats from the other so-called weapons of mass destruction, namely chemical and nuclear/radiological materials. The threat from biological terrorism to humans clarifies for the global village the nature and harsh reality of the new world community. The threat overlaps with agricultural, fishery and veterinary populations and, as such, could be said to represent a threat to the entire biosphere.

Dealing with biological issues necessitates the protection of our civil society through strict measures, for example, the possible need for quarantine restrictions on the few to save the lives of many. The movement of diseases across national borders requires new relationships between nation states and possibly even new areas of the world. Lastly, the psychological impact in terms of the fear and terror from a biological event will test the entire civil structure and has, in its own right, morbidity and mortality implications.

The attacks that occurred on the September 11, 2001, marked in the words of George W. Bush, the President of the United States, the first war of the 21st Century. If he is right then what we also saw was the new face of war in the 21st Century, a war fought using principles established very early in the annals of military history and a war that will require the United States to rapidly adapt to the new threat— this is an asymmetric war in which the attacker will seek to attack and exploit the weaknesses in the United States defenses. The concern now must be to ascertain in a concise way the extent of those weaknesses, to address them in an appropriate and effective manner and ensure that what are now weaknesses are future strengths— it will be important for the future of the country to make the work of the terrorist as difficult as possible. One area of perceived weakness and thus an area of concern is the threat posed by biological weapons. A biological attack, in particular, poses a special concern, because such an event would almost certainly have more serious national and international ramifications than a comparable attack with any other weapon, and because managing a biological crisis raises uniquely difficult and complex issues beyond those faced in other large-scale disasters. Several analysts, including the authors of this article, have remained consistent in warning that, despite a publicly documented vulnerability to this increasing asymmetric threat, the United States has no national strategy or plan for dealing with a potentially catastrophic terrorist event, no national structure for carrying out such a strategy, and no established procedures to help national leaders prepare to guide the country through such a crisis.

The absence of such a strategy is all the more surprising given the significant, and almost unimaginable consequences of a coordinated biological attack. This despite the predicted low probability of a biological attack being undertaken in a successful manner by a terrorist group.

There is no reliable way to predict when, how, or if such an event will occur, but the technology of mass destruction and disruption using biological agents exists, and there are those in the world angry enough and fanatical enough and violent enough to use it. We should not let ourselves be ruled by our fears, but we cannot responsibly ignore the danger or fail to take steps to meet it. This is especially the case following the escalation of terrorist actions that were manifest on September 11th— the attacks on that day can be described as mass terrorism. They were designed not merely to terrorize but also to kill citizens of the United States in a deliberate act of war on the sovereign state of the country. Such escalation marks the dawn of a new age in terrorism and provides a chilling view of at least one version of the coming wars in the 21st Century. If biological weapons become part of that new warfare we must be prepared, our preparedness will contribute to decreasing the threat— uncertainty in the mind of a potential attacker as to the effect of the attack may deter them from using that weapon, if we remove all the "easy options" we make waging war through terrorism a means that may be too much effort for the "reward" and thus provide deterrence as a component of our armory of protective capabilities.

Biological Attacks

The threat from biological attacks is characterized by these criteria:

- They are manmade and deliberate with a potential to target human, agricultural and animal populations;

- They threaten or inflict casualties in very large numbers: deaths, injuries or illness at a level that would almost certainly overwhelm local or state health or agriculture systems unless their efforts can be quickly reinforced with massive additional resources and medical and veterinary personnel; these additional resources themselves will then be subject to quarantine and possible infection;

- They may require imposing isolation or quarantine restrictions to prevent infected persons or animals from spreading disease or to allow for administration of appropriate medical countermeasures; even if such measures might lead to exposure of unexposed persons or animals who happen to be within the contaminated area;

- They cause or pose a risk of panic and disruption of economic and community life on a scale that would significantly threaten public order;

- They threaten or cause economic damage grave enough to cause widespread hardship and serious harm to the national economy, and the disruption of global financial stability;

- As a result of all or some combination of these factors, they have the capacity to weaken democratic institutions and beliefs, undermine legal protection of civil liberties, and damage the relationship between the American people and their government and its ability to provide international leadership.

The Unique Nature of Bioterrorism

Bioterrorism, or the deliberate release of biological agents for purposes of disruption and destruction, is different from other means of asymmetric mass destruction. An effective national response requires a national plan that must consider the special character of such an attack and the additional elements that will be needed for a successful response. Factors to be considered include:

- The primary responders to an attack by chemical, radiation, or conventional weapons will be public safety agencies— fire departments, police, hazardous material control teams. In a biological attack, the health or agriculture systems will have the leading role. This does not necessitate a separate leader at the national level, but extensive public health input will be needed in developing a strategy for mass-destruction events involving biological agents. In the absence of an existing national plan, hospitals and county and state health agencies around the country are developing separate protocols for bioterrorism preparedness. Any federal preparedness plan will have to address these efforts.

- Mitigating the effects of a release may require isolation or quarantine of those exposed or potentially exposed to a disease agent. The number of individuals to be isolated may be extremely large and their confinement may be for an extended time, depending on the incubation period for a specific agent. It may be necessary to prohibit all entry or exit from the area of an incident. It is even conceivable that the United States mainland will have to be closed to all international travel. While that may sound overdramatic, the present struggle with foot-and-mouth disease in Europe shows that even such draconian measures may not be too far-fetched to think

- The available medical countermeasures for some of the most probable biological agents are not in routine clinical use. Therefore, medical personnel treating bioterror victims may have to use medicines whose safety and efficacy are unproven or supported only by limited data. Special legal instruments may be needed to permit use of these medicines in a crisis. Not only legal but substantial ethical and moral concerns as well will arise from the need to treat large numbers of people who are not only endangered by the target disease but may be at risk from the use of the medicine itself.

- Because an introduced disease can be spread from the point of release by people who are infected but do not yet show symptoms, the response by health and public safety authorities may have to extend to a large geographic area—moreover, an area whose exact boundaries may not be known immediately or for some time after an attack. This will raise management and logistical problems well beyond those with other mass-destruction weapons, whose effects will occur in a much more easily predictable area.

A particularly important task within any plan will be to maintain liaison with relevant government and non-government agencies abroad. Biological and other potential weapons of mass destruction are not limited by international boundaries, and neither are those— whether organized groups or angry "lone wolves"— who might use them. Also vital will be the task of building public understanding and support. Establishing credibility with the public and with the news media before an event occurs is the best way to avoid inaccurate, panicky, irresponsible reporting when the crisis comes. The process of developing a plan should be conducted as openly as possible and a special effort should be made not only to inform the public and media as a plan takes shape, but also to include media representatives in realistic training exercises. Further, this approach should help identify key resources that can deliver reliable and authoritative data and advice in the event of a bioterrorism incident.

In developing a plan to deal with the threat from a biological attack the strategy should take into account that a traumatic event can take a heavy psychological toll not only on victims, but also on the public safety and other emergency personnel who are the front-line responders to a crisis. Plans for dealing with a major terrorist incident should have a component on meeting the psychological needs of those victims and responders.

Among the many difficult administrative, legal, and philosophical issues that will need to be addressed— and that may require new regulations or laws— are such questions as:

- Reconciling and coordinating the tasks, responsibilities, powers, and jurisdiction of literally hundreds of federal, state, and local agencies;

- Reinforcing the health care (or agricultural/veterinary/fisheries) system to deal with mass casualties;

- Resolving legal uncertainties and establishing clear and effective procedures to impose and enforce quarantine regulations and the need for mass prophylactic treatment;

- Clarifying legal and other issues connected with the use of U.S. military forces within the United States to help maintain civil order and meet a public health emergency;

- Dealing with extraordinarily intensive media coverage and finding ways to inform the public honestly but without contributing to panic;

- Reconciling emergency medical and public health procedures or safeguards against cyberterrorism with constitutional protections of privacy.

In the opinion of the authors the concerns go beyond the issue of dealing with the loss, or potential loss, of life and property, resulting from a catastrophic terrorist attack. In such an event, the structures, values, traditions, and principles of a democratic society will be put at risk too. As well as considering how to prepare for and respond to the immediate emergency, we also have a responsibility to think about how we can best protect those structures and values, preserve civil society and constitutional rights, and maintain the mutual respect and trust between the government and governed that is essential for a living democracy. The authors believe that the level of public trust in its leadership will have an enormous, perhaps decisive, impact on the government's ability to manage a crisis successfully and on our society's ability to survive it without serious damage to democratic institutions and beliefs. It should also be self-evident that once a crisis begins, it will be too late for leaders to start trying to build that trust. For that reason, thinking about how to plan for a catastrophic event should be a compelling reminder that the time to keep the public's trust is before that event occurs. A broad commitment to policies of responsibility and openness by the national leadership, in all aspects of governing, may not appear in so many words in any specific disaster plan. But it is vital to our preparation, just as it is in all aspects of national policy and leadership.

The specific areas of concern that need to addressed include:

- Medical Response
- Public Investment in Critical Infrastructure

Medical Response

In respect of the specific issue of medical response the major conclusions included the following:

- The quality and timeliness of the medical response is the most important element in determining the outcome for the victims of a terrorist event.

- Provision of the best possible medical response is thus a critical element in planning to mitigate a terrorist event.

- Medical response planning cannot be added after the event if it is to influence the outcome for the victims. It must be an integral part of the plan from the outset, it must be widely discussed and everyone who is involved should understand their individual roles and responsibilities.

Within the area of medical response lies the critical area of public health management. The ability to defend against the threat posed by biological agents will be greatly enhanced by an effective public health system. The effective implementation of these tools prior to an event will be the critical determinant in the outcome of a biological attack that targets a human population.

The basic tools for public health management comprise:

- Infrastructure
  - Recognition & response
  - Vaccination & treatment
  - Isolation & infection control

- Enabling legislation
  - Public law
  - Specific regulations
- Training

The lack of these tools in any population ensures that the people remain vulnerable and that diseases can proliferate unseen and largely untreated. They also allow a biological attack to develop to the level of a significant problem before detection and action can be taken. Unfortunately reversing the neglect of the last quarter of a century will not occur overnight. There will need to be a coordinated, i.e. managed, funded and resourced, effort to take effective action and repair the damaged infrastructure. Of course, some of the neglect came about because of advances in medicine that meant that we were better able to treat diseases— the advent of the antibiotic era and the tremendous successes that the use of antibiotics provided in disease management contributed to the demise of the public health initiatives. But the very tools that took us to a new level in disease control are now failing us in terms of naturally-occurring diseases, the incidence of infectious disease is no longer falling at the previous rate and we are now facing antibiotic-resistance organisms that have "made our hospitals their home"— in the United States over 19,000 persons admitted to hospitals develop a disease infection in the hospital that results in death. These "nosocomial" (hospital-acquired) diseases, the health management problems that they create and the resultant loss of life, are a harbinger of what some biological agents may inflict on a country if they were to be released.

The past 25 years have seen the Public Health Service (PHS) in the United States reduced to a level that is only just above functional operation. Any crisis, including the annual influenza outbreaks, shows the strain that the PHS personnel are operating under and it is only by truly dedicated efforts of those staff that the crisis is kept to a level that is manageable. There is however, no guarantee that the future will be as kind and that the types of disease and number of infected persons will remain at levels that can be managed. Whilst the absence of any meaningful public health system is a significant contributory factor to the onward march of diseases that we can otherwise treat with adequate resources, there exists a threat that could overwhelm any capability— even that of a so-called modern healthcare system. The threat from so-called emerging (and the newly-termed reemerging) diseases is truly a major concern. The emergence of new diseases such as West Nile Virus, Sin Nombre Virus and the re-emergence of diseases like Tuberculosis (TB) and the variant, multiple-drug resistant TB, represent true challenges to our health system and even our national security. Furthermore, in parts of the United States, for example the U.S.— Mexico Border Region, the health status of the population is such that the health system has already broken down (not that there was much of a system to speak of in the first place) and the diseases that are now prevalent in the Border Region represent a real threat and hazard to the population of the United States. The migration of workers from that region into the main body of the United States brings with it those same diseases— diseases know no borders. There is no doubt in the mind of the authors of this article that there needs to be an immediate review of our current systems and an injection of resources to establish a baseline of public health activity that is commensurate with the growing threat— regardless of whether that threat is posed by border health issues, emerging or reemerging diseases or bioterrorism. To fail to act would be to invite trouble— and no-one wishes to be at home when "Mr. Trouble" starts calling.

Public Investment in Critical Infrastructure

There is a significant problem with implementing such strategies in the United States, the shift from a publicly-funded to a privately-funded healthcare system means that significant elements that would be critical to an effective public health response are now in the private sector of the industry. This will require that any federally-funded plan includes a compensation or reimbursement for costs incurred by the private sector in supporting the efforts of the Government. This will include not only the costs of specific medications, but also the costs of additional training, licensing and accreditation of the medical personnel. Furthermore, if the plan requires that there is an excess capacity requirement, that would be used under conditions of extremis, the cost of such resource will also have to be borne by the Government. The true cost of the shift from a public to a private medical system is now becoming apparent. While there has been improvement in some elements of patient care, the cost has been considerable. The investment by private industry in the current healthcare system is designed to meet the requirements for the customer base in a very tightly controlled manner. The private funding organizations have no need for excess resources, they operate at levels very close to minimal unless there is a means by which the cost of the additional capability can be reimbursed by insurance. These organizations, whilst recognizing the need and sympathizing with the problem, cannot and will not burden themselves or their customers with the cost of maintaining a system that would meet the Government's needs in respect of biological agents that pose a threat to the national security. The cost of a system that was capable of meeting the consequences of even the smallest of bioterrorist action will be considerable and require coverage of a broad range of possible agents. Specific examples of the resources (costs) involved include:

- Surveillance and Epidemiology Capability

- Rapid Diagnosis Capability

- Specialist Drugs and Vaccines

- Training and Education

- Redundancy in Patient-Facilities and Specialist Equipment

- Quarantine and/or Isolation Facilities

One option for the Government would be the use of military facilities under the management and guidance of the Department of Veteran Affairs. This has certain attractions but it is worth noting that the VA operates a very "thin" capability, matching its resources to the needs of its "customers" in a tightly controlled manner, and that the VA must continue to treat the current recipients of TriCare that rely on its service for their routine health needs. The amount of excess capacity in the military system is thus minimal and probably of only limited use in a civilian scenario with more than a few dozen cases. Nonetheless, this system is easily quantified, relatively easy to access, and has personnel already knowledgeable about the likely biological (and chemical) agents that might be the basis for an attack.

One valuable by-product of any increase in the capability of the public health system will be an improvement in the ability of the nation to intervene when the attacker is not a terrorist but is "Mother Nature" herself. We are increasingly vulnerable to emerging and reemerging disease states and continue to develop new problems through our abuse of current technology. For example, the indiscriminate use of antibiotics in the veterinary and agricultural markets has meant that the increase in the incidence of antibiotic-resistant diseases is reaching staggering proportions. The rate at which the bacterial populations, both good and bad, are able to acquire or develop resistance capability is increasing. For example, within six months of the formal market launch of the latest class of antibiotics there are reports of resistant strains of bacteria, including bacteria that the antibiotic was not even targeting. Given that it currently takes on average, twelve years to get from the laboratory to the launch of a new antibiotic product we are fighting a losing battle if the bacteria are able to defeat the product inside of the first year of market launch. We must review the situation and develop an effective strategy for future use or be prepared to operate our healthcare system in a manner akin to that which existed prior to the advent of antibiotics. The choices will not be simple but to fail to act is to invite trouble.

How Real Is the Threat from Bioterrorism?

There is no doubt that in a world in which there are increasing divisions based on geo-political, religious and economic schisms the battle-space, or area of conflict, is becoming more and more indistinct. The opposing factions are no longer the armies, navies and air forces of the proponents but now include the civilian populations. Future conflicts may not be "staged" on battlefields but will become rooted in our cities. In fact it could be argued that the greatest forces on earth are now those that can be unleashed by the civilian in terms of voting power and consumerism. The simple fact is that civilians are now considered "legitimate" targets rather than the poor unfortunate victims of "collateral damage" during military operations. In this changed framework of conflict the types of weapon will also change and evolve to "better fit" the goals of the adversaries. In this context weapons of mass destruction or disruption (WMD) will likely play an increasing role. That is not to say that there will not be considerable casualties resulting from the use of conventional weapons and "one-off" devices involving explosives, such as that used to destroy the U.S. Embassies in East Africa or to attack the USS Cole, but these types of device are relatively easy to defend against if one is prepared to accept limitations and restrictions on access to likely target sites. The incidents of September 11th demonstrated how, through a lateral jump in the modus operandi of terrorism, a "known" threat (a hijacked airliner) could be used to devastating effect in destroying symbols of a country's strength and kill and maim thousands of citizens.

One reason why the terrorists were able to complete their attack was the belief held up until the first three "crashes" that hijackers intended to walk away from the hijacked aircraft. When it was clear that this was no longer a "rational conclusion" the passengers on the remaining hijacked airliner appear to have decided to take the matter into their own hands with dramatic consequences for their heroism. It can be assumed that any hijacker of an airliner in the future cannot anticipate that the passengers will remain passive and that the tactic used to such devastating effect on the World Trade Center Towers and the Pentagon will not be as simple. The type of act seen last September 11th is probably best characterized as mass terrorism; it can radically alter the status of both the attacking agent/terrorist group and the country that is attacked. The totality of the attack on the World Trade Center Towers and the Pentagon is still not clear, but the immediate after effects in terms of loss of life, disruption to local operations, economic damage and perhaps most critically the psychological effect on an entire nation are all too apparent to the whole world. The other aspect of the latest attack is the "raising of the terror threshold" for future attacks. It is a sad fact that for each terrorist event there is a threshold that must be crossed to gain exposure in the world's press—as the press and public become inured to each event the threshold for the next event appears to increase. Thus the events of September 11th have now set the threshold for the next "world's worst act of terror"—in some ways compelling the would-be world's worst terrorist to even more inhuman acts and to larger targets. The prospect of an individual attack targeting more than the tens of thousands housed in the World Trade Center Towers and the Pentagon is difficult to comprehend unless one considers the possible use of WMD. For this reason alone it must now be considered that the liklihood that a terrorist group will seek to acquire and use WMD has increased by a substantial amount.

Of course an increase in the probability of acquisition does not translate into an equal increase in the probability of success in the application and use of such weapons. There remain a number of significant hurdles between acquisition and employment. One function that increased preparedness provides is to make the successful use of the weapons less certain, i.e., as the level of defensive capability increases, the chance of an attack succeeding decreases. This basic relationship can be shifted to such a degree that it makes the use of some WMD material of no real value— thus acting as a significant deterrent. In the language of asymmetry what was once a weakness, and thus a target, is now a strength and offers little advantage to a potential attacker. In terms of the specific agents of potential biological warfare or bioterrorism there is an added benefit. With implementation of the countermeasures comes the added value of providing the public health system with tools that will enhance the defense against emerging and reemerging diseases and the possibility of using the very same systems to track diseases that are naturally-occurring and which are entering the country at the borders. This concept of national security through health policy is the basic tenet that supported the creation of the National Security Health Policy Center at the Potomac Institute For Policy Studies, the present address of the authors of this article.

Responding to Mass Terrorist Attacks: The Psychological Imperative

George S. Everly, Jr.

An Act of War!

As this paper is being written, the United States is enmeshed in a new war, a war against terrorism. National Guard troops stand vigilant in airports throughout the United States. American soldiers in Uzbekistan support a military action against Afghanistan. Gunboats guard our harbors. Yet, the war is being conducted against an enemy who remains ill-defined, stealthily cloaked, and who has already breached the outer perimeter of our homeland defenses now lying in wait to wage the next attack. Osama bin Laden, suspected terrorist mastermind, released a video tape soon after the military action against Afghanistan began, indicating that the terrorist attacks against the United States will continue. The likelihood of such an occurrence certainly approximates 100%. At stake in this war are the lives of soldiers, the lives of civilians, and everyday life as we know it. At stake in this war is the future of our children, the future of our nation. Despite the mobilization of military and other resources, however, we stand under-prepared to wage this war from an imperative perspective, i.e., the psychological perspective. As the military guards our shores, who guards our sense of psychological security and vitality?

On September 11, 2001 at approximately 8:45 am the hijacked American Airlines Flight 11 en route from Boston crashed into the north tower at the World Trade Center in New York City. Shortly thereafter, at 9:06 am, the hijacked United Airlines Flight 175 crashed into the remaining south tower. At 10:00 am, the south tower collapsed sending a wave of debris for blocks and trapping hundreds of firefighters and law enforcement officers who had rushed to rescue those working in the tower. At 10:29 am, the north tower also collapsed.

Approximately 55 minutes after the World Trade Center was attacked, a similar terrorist attack was perpetrated against the Pentagon in Washington, D.C. American Airlines Flight 77 en route from the Washington Dulles Airport to Los Angeles crashed into the Pentagon as an apparent secondary target after possibly intending to crash into the White House.

Although the resultant physical devastation and physical human suffering was beyond anything this nation has ever experienced, the psychological devastation may not be known for years, perhaps even for generations!

There can be no doubt that acts of terrorism engender a large-scale psychological morbidity. In fact, the explicit goal of any true act of terrorism is to create a condition of extreme fear, uncertainty, demoralization, and helplessness, i.e., "terror." The direct target of the terrorist act, therefore, is never the actual target by design, rather it is but the means to an end. In the cases of terrorism, the "psychological casualties" will always outnumber the "physical casualties."

In the wake of a terrorist attack, physicians can physically immunize and treat those who require such attention. Engineers can reconstruct buildings and roads. But who rebuilds the essence of humanity which has been violently ripped away from those who suffered the terrorist attack? How do we reconstruct a belief in justice and safety in the wake of a mass terrorist attack? Without attention to the "psychological side of terrorism," we run the risk of rebuilding a city without a spirit, without a vitality, without a sense of humanity.

Any effective response to such crises must mandate psychological intervention, as well as physical crisis intervention. As an example, the Defense Against Weapons of Mass Destruction Act of 1996 (Senators Nunn, Lugar & Domenici) mandates the enhancement of domestic preparedness and response capabilities in the wake of attacks against the United States using weapons of mass destruction (WMD). Although a small component, provisions are made for psychological crisis intervention with both emergency responders and primary civilian victim populations.

Understanding the Threat

There exist three credible and significant threats to our nation at this time, based upon the most recent of current events as described above:

- the objective threat of incidents of physical destruction and death;

- the perceived threat of injury/death to individuals, families, and communities;

- the threat of sociological upheaval; and

- the threat of economic recession, with the potential for specific industrial sectors to collapse.

Logistically, it seems a low probability event that groups of terrorists could defeat our nation militarily. However, a higher probability event would be that the terrorists could cripple our nation to such a degree that they achieve desired political and foreign policy victories. How could such an outcome occur? The answer rests upon understanding that three of the four threats described above are actually psychological in nature. Fear, albeit subjective, is an agent of change. It can destroy one's personal health through excessive stress. It can split apart families. It can split apart communities and destroy political unity. It can destroy businesses, and cause economic collapse (as evidenced by the technology crash).

The attack on September 11, 2001, was obviously different than the attack on the World Trade Center perpetrated eight years earlier. The amount of physical destruction and the loss of life are clearly incomparable. However, the psychological destruction is incomparable, as well. In the wake of the first attack on the World Trade Center, the illusion of safety was largely maintained by the American people. This was largely so even in the wake of the terrorist attack upon the Federal Building in Oklahoma City. This author noted less a sense of vulnerability, and more a sense of anger. However, the September 11th attack upon the World Trade Center has left America scarred, but more importantly the September 11th attacks have left the American people in an intolerable state, a state of psychological vulnerability. As this author walked the streets of Manhattan anger, fear, disbelief, and disorientation were all in evidence. Both high school children and adults alike, however, could be heard to occasionally voice apprehension and even objection to the notion of "retaliation" against the terrorists in hopes they would cease their acts of terrorism. Even more interestingly, some individuals voiced their concern as to what we did to "deserve" these acts of coordinated brutality. "Victim self-blame" is not an uncommon response in individuals who have been traumatized.

As if following a script crafted by the terrorists, America came to a screeching halt seemingly obsessed with the up-to-the-minute news reports of the carnage. Later, just as we contemplated shifting from rescue to recovery at the World Trade Center's "ground zero," the American stock markets dropped far beyond European declines and far beyond the estimates of many financial experts. Ever more evidence that the world's most influential financial markets are but slaves of the human psyche. Clearly, the legacy of the September 11th attacks on America, at this point in time, is fear, i.e., the fear, perhaps even terror for some, associated with the anticipation of the next terrorist attack. Many believe that the probability of such a retaliatory attack is 100%. We must act as if such is true.

Three Phases of Terrorism

There are three fundamental phases to an act of terrorism from society's perspective:

The Pre-Attack, Pre-Crisis Phase

This, by definition, is the time period prior to the actual attack. There are three functions which are to be performed during this phase:

(1) Threat assessment, performed by law enforcement, military, and intelligence community resources.

(2) Prevention, performed by law enforcement, military, and intelligence community resources.

(3) Psychological preparation of the primary and secondary target populations, as well as emergency services populations.

We believe that the better prepared the population, especially the emergency services population, the less severe the malignancy, the less severe the overall impact of the attack. It seems clear, we have not instituted adequate psychological preparatory mechanisms. The alternative argument to some form of psychological preparation would be the use of denial as a psychological defense. Psychological denial entails simply ignoring any terrorist threat as irrelevant. This conforms to the "ignorance is bliss" philosophy. In the absence of terrorism, it is effective. When the terrorism is isolated and personally removed, it is effective. When the terrorism becomes real for the person/society, denial may serve to actually enhance subsequent feelings of betrayal, vulnerability, and fear.

The Acute Event Management Phase

This phase persists as long as event assessment, containment, rescue, and recovery efforts continue. In this phase, communications, fire suppression, law enforcement, emergency medical, and other rescue and recovery personnel perform their respective functions. Emergency mental health personnel provide acute psychological support and crisis intervention services. Techniques such as "crisis management briefings" (Everly, 2000), defusings, demobilizations, and individual crisis intervention/crisis counseling within the integrated "critical incident stress management" (CISM) system (Everly, Flannery, Eyler, & Mitchell, 2001) may be implemented. Disaster emergency mental health activities are not recognized as useful by all mental health practitioners, however (see Mitchell & Everly, 2001 for a review). Some express concern that early psychological intervention could be injurious to victims of terrorism; thus some suggest postponing intervention for several weeks and then implementing psychotherapy. Certainly any mental health intervention must be implemented cautiously, and there is risk associated with all forms of medical or psychological intervention, including psychotherapy. Anyone who spent time at "ground zero" in New York during the rescue and recovery processes, as did the author, or anyone who even saw the pictures of the primary victims, the victim's family members, or the emergency services personnel would likely agree that there was a need for some form of emergency psychological support. Similar emergency psychological intervention models have been implemented in Kuwait City, after the Iraqi invasion, in Croatia after the civil war, in and Oklahoma City after the bombing. The American Red Cross in cooperation with the American Psychological Association has developed and effectively implemented a national disaster mental health network which has responded to every major disaster in the United States since 1992. But the origin of emergency mental health functions can even be traced back to the military efforts in the two great World Wars. Had such efforts at emergency psychological support proved harmful, surely they would have been discontinued decades ago.

The Consequence Management and Reconstruction Phase

Once most acts of heroism have been performed, once the psychological "shock" has melted away, profound frustration, anxiety, grief, disillusionment, mourning, and depression fully emerge. This is the phase wherein the engineers may rebuild the physical aspects of the city. But, it is within this phase that the mental health personnel must take center stage to facilitate the recovery process, facilitate a process of psychological reconstruction, in effect, rebuild the psychological aspects of the city, state and country.

From an emergency mental health perspective, a multi-faceted emergency mental health intervention is recommended to facilitate the quest for psychological reconstruction.

The achievement of psychological reconstruction is the operational imperative. Without a sense of psychological closure, without the ability to move on in life, the terrorists will prevail. Without the ability to successfully mourn our dead, memorialize our heroes, and continue to grow as individuals, families, communities, and as a nation, the terrorists will win. The traditional mental health system as it exists now seems ill-prepared to meet the forthcoming challenges, especially in light of retaliatory terrorism subsequent to the military actions in Afghanistan.

The potential problems associated with providing an adequate mental health response to the psychological warfare we have just entered are three-fold: first, not all psychologists, psychiatrists, and social workers are adequately trained to provide emergency mental health services; second, confounding countertransference reactions may prevent those who are trained from delivering effective mental health services, emergent or otherwise, and third, given the diversity of targets for terrorism, the members of the mental health community, as well as the physical health community, may become primary victims themselves, thus further reducing the available resources.

Thus, it may be argued that we must not only bolster our professional mental resources through enhanced technical training in the provision of trauma related services, but we need to train mental health paraprofessionals to deliver emergency mental health services and to provide psychological triaging functions.

In addition, we need to implement social psychological principles so as to facilitate a condition of psychological resiliency to terrorism.

Recommendations to Enhance Psychological Resiliency

(1)   Never lose sight of the fact that either as a primary or secondary goal, the terrorist act is designed to engender psychological instability. More specifically, the goal of the terrorist act is to induce a state of psychological uncertainty, personal vulnerability, and fear, i.e., terror. Terrorism is psychological warfare!

(2)   Remember, once the terrorist act has been perpetrated, it is the resultant state of mind held by the target population and its leadership which functionally serves to augment, or to mitigate, the actual severity of the terrorist action. Psychological support and the restoration of a sense of community is imperative. Establish crisis intervention hot-lines and walk-in crisis intervention facilities in every community directly or indirectly affected, as the need arises.

(3)   Consider, the psychological state of mind of emergency responders and military personnel will have direct effects upon their ability to perform their necessary functions and upon the physical and mental health of the targeted population, as well. Provide pre-incident psychological resiliency training as well as on-going psychological support during and after the terrorist attack. Include families in all aspects of these important processes.

(4)   Collaborate with mass media services to provide on-going information to all involved and affected populations. Credible information is anxiolytic, and contradicts the sense of chaos. Information combats destructive rumors. Don't forget the children. Go to their schools and provide reassurance. Schools should provide structured times that are set aside to discuss relevant current events with the aim to providing a ventilation of feelings, as well as providing a venue for rumor control. Provide age-appropriate reading, mass media, and community activities to help children cope with the situation. Limit media exposure to those sources that are constructively informative. Limit the amount of news exposure for children. Parents may wish to provide structured time at home to discuss current events as well. Information is power!

(5) Take whatever steps seem requisite to re-establish a sense of physical safety for the public. Communicate these efforts as security considerations will allow. Special considerations should be made for children, the elderly, and the infirmed.

(6) Enlist the support of political, educational, medical, economic, and religious leaders to facilitate communications, calm fears, provide personal crisis intervention (if adequately trained to do so), and instill hope. Structured community meetings may be utilized. Take advantage of venues that already attract groups of individuals to impart information and develop community cohesion.

(7) Re-establish normal communication, transportation, school, and work schedules as soon as possible. The longer and greater the disruption, the greater the perceived risk and lack of safety on the part of the public.

(8) Understand and utilize the power of symbols as a means of re-establishing community cohesion. Flags, bumper stickers, signs, and billboards can all be effective.

(9) Initiate rituals to honor the survivors, honor the rescuers, and honor the dead. Provide opportunities for others, not directly affected, to assist those directly affected, e.g., donations of blood, food, clothing, money, etc.

(10) Communicate to all the notion that an effective way to honor the dead is to carry on and succeed in life. To do otherwise is to allow the terrorists to be victorious.

Summary

Terrorism is psychological warfare. This is a war that is won, not on a battlefield, but in the mind. The sophistication of the mental health services may be as important a factor in winning the war against terrorism as any other resource a nation may possess. The challenges, therefore, emerge as:

- Mobilizing a network of mental health professionals specially trained in disaster mental health and the treatment of traumatic syndromes.

- Constructing a mass media strategy to enhance social cohesion.

- Using existing resources as platforms for community planning, e.g., religious facilities, schools, etc.

- Encouraging continued economic growth.

- Using psychological resources to enhance the effectiveness of military responses to terrorism, e.g., "understanding the enemy."

- Integrating psychological resources in an overall plan to enhance the perception of safety and stability.

References

Everly, G.S., Jr., (2000). Crisis management briefings: Large group crisis intervention in response to terrorism, disasters, and violence. International Journal of Emergency Mental Health, 2, 53-57.

Everly, G.S., Jr. & Lating, J.M. (in press). Personality-guided treatment of posttraumatic stress disorder (PTSD): A practical guide for clinicians. Wash.D.C.: American Psychological Assn.

Everly, G.S., Jr., Flannery, R.B., Jr., Eyler, V., &, Mitchell, J. (2001). Sufficiency analysis of an integrated multicomponent approach to crisis intervention. Advances in Mind-Body Medicine, 17, 174-183.

Mitchell, J.T. & Everly, G.S., Jr. (2001). Critical Incident Stress Debriefing (CISD). An operations manual for group crisis intervention. Ellicott City, MD: Chevron.

The Probability of Bioterrorism in the United States

Stephen Prior

The most important questions of life are indeed, for the most part, really only problems of probability.

Pierre Simon Laplace, Théorie Analytique des Probabilités, 1812

Probability is expectation founded upon partial knowledge. A perfect acquaintance with all the circumstances affecting the occurrence of an event would change expectation into certainty, and leave neither room nor demand for a theory of probabilities.

George Boole, An Investigation of the Law of Thought

One of the consequences of the events of September 11, 2001, is a widespread concern on the part of the public to the possibility of further attacks on the United States involving biological agents in acts of terrorism. This is in part born out of the realization that the "homeland" is now considered a terrorist target and that for certain terrorist groups there are no moral or ethical barriers to the slaughter of innocent civilians using such heinous weapons. It is true to say that while there is no reliable way to predict when, how, or if such an event will occur, the fact remains that the technology of mass destruction and disruption using biological agents exists and may be an attractive proposition for those seeking the "downfall" of the United States. So how can the probability of such an event be predicted with any degree of accuracy? And how is it that there is such divergent opinion between supposed "experts"?

In the aftermath of the events of September 11th there was considerable debate about the likelihood or probability of an attack using biological weapons. One explanation for the diverse opinions is that the experts offering their views were addressing two separate, but linked, probabilities. It is clear that consideration of the probability of a bioterrorist event being attempted can be analyzed separately from consideration of the probability of any one event of attaining a stated goal. It is possible to envision scenarios in which the probability of an attempt is high but the probability of successfully attaining the stated goal remains low because of barriers to effective implementation.

Furthermore it is possible that if there is only a very limited possibility of a proposed attack attaining its intended goal, or that an ineffective attack may invoke an unwelcome response, the perpetrator may decide not to attack using a weapon of dubious effectiveness. Thus opinions on the "probability of a bioterrorist attack" may be very different to the opinions on the "probability of a successful attack". (Authors note: In either case the probability of infection by a bioterrorist event for any person residing in the United States remains exceedingly low, certainly well below the probability of being injured through everyday events such as automobile accidents).

The probability of a bioterrorist attack at the present time is also reduced by the fact that in the current situation the heightened awareness of the possible vulnerability of the United States to further terrorist action has resulted in an increase in overall security measures, including those that will impact the possible use of biological agents. It is a widely held belief that one function that such increased preparedness provides is to make the successful use of the weapons less certain, i.e., as the level of defensive capability increases the chance of an attack succeeding decreases.

As stated above an increase in the probability of acquisition does not translate into an equal increase in the probability of success in the application and use of such weapons. In the case of biological weapons there remain a number of significant hurdles between acquisition and employment. It is beyond the scope of this paper, and inappropriate at this time, to examine in detail the hurdles and the extent to which those seeking to utilize biological agents may overcome them but certain general conclusions can be stated.

The Biological Weapons Spectrum

The potential spectrum or range of biological agents (toxins, bacteria, viruses, etc.) that could constitute biological weapons has been described in detail in various articles and will not be repeated herein. There are however several factors that separate the "class of agents" from the "class of weapons". The most significant of these is a technology for effective delivery or dissemination. Any use of a biological "weapon" requires that the "agent" is delivered or disseminated using a system that will allow for subsequent action (infection) by the biological agent. Such systems can be as complex as high-pressure sprayers or specially-designed bombs, or as simple as contaminating food—the number of persons infected being defined by the conditions of release and environmental factors such as wind dispersion, agent dilution and inactivation, and other defined variables. For most agents the amount of dissemination will define the extent of infection, i.e., only those directly exposed, and in receipt of an infectious (or challenge) dose will develop the disease.

For a very few agents, those that cause contagious disease, the extent of dissemination will also depend on the extent of contact that an infected individual has with non-infected persons during the period of the disease state when they are "infectious." The range of agents that are in this category is quite small and includes many agents that are susceptible to current treatments such as antibiotics. One exception to the ease of treatment is smallpox (Variola major). This highly infectious disease constitutes some people's "nightmare bioterrorist weapon." Fortunately, the acquisition of the agent of smallpox is a very difficult undertaking requiring access to stocks that are considered to be under the strictest control (only the USA and Russia have declared stocks of the virus and these are under strict control). Overall it is clear that selecting a suitable bioweapon is not simply a matter of picking the "best disease"— getting from the selected agent to an effective weapon also represents a potentially significant barrier to any putative bioterrorist the development of a "biological capability" is discussed below.

The Capability Curve

The capability to acquire, produce and deliver biological weapons has been variously described as being simple, requiring little more than a "brave man and a bathtub", moderately difficult, requiring the skills of a graduate scientist, and difficult, requiring the support or sponsorship of a State active in such research. The fact is that all of the above statements are true in part— the extent of the required capability will depend on your intended goals. It is clear that acquisition, production and delivery of small quantities of some biological agents can be achieved and has resulted in human infection, a good example of such action being the attack by an Oregon-based cult using Salmonella in 1984. The level of sophistication was low and a large number of people were sick as a result of the action but this is not the type of nightmare attack that the nation currently fears. If we consider one of those scenarios, the acquisition of a smallpox weapon, we are looking at a "whole new ball game". In fact if we pursue the baseball analogy we are talking about the difference in capability in the bioterrorism arena between the Oregon attack constituting a "pick-up game of softball" and the putative smallpox attack being "the final game in the World Series". They both involve teams playing baseball but whereas many people could participate in the "softball" game only a very few, those with experience, talent and a support system, can make the "World Series". This relationship between the ability to effectively undertake a "mass bioterrorist event" and biological capability is shown in the graphic below:

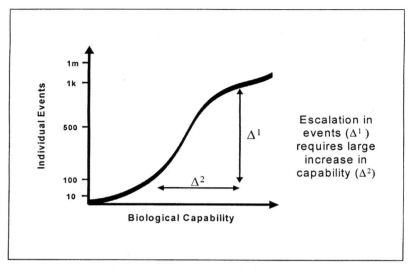

As stated above the elements that specify biological capability will not be discussed in this paper. It is however a truism that the "brave man (and his bathtub)" are to be found in the lower left corner. The capability and facilities required to get to the top right portion of the graphic are more akin to those of a pharmaceutical manufacturing plant complete with trained and skilled operatives.

The capability required to shift from a "small-scale" event to a "mass-event" is a significant barrier to any potential perpetrator. In fact, it is the opinion of the author that very few laboratories have the "know-how" to climb the curve described by Δ^1 and Δ^2 and that for most terrorist groups the gap could only be closed by their receiving "state-sponsorship". Thus our efforts to prevent a potential attack on the United States should include clear statements about the reprisals that would result if anyone is found to have provided such sponsorship or capability to any terrorist group.

The Fickle Face of "Mother Nature"

Even if our putative bioterrorist manages to select a "suitable" agent and has the knowledge and experience to climb the capability curve to the point where the resultant biological weapon is a viable option there remains one barrier to its potential use. How does the bioterrorist prevent himself from becoming a victim? If we posit that the agent has only limited capability to spread we can also posit that the same agent, unless widely-disseminated, will have only relatively local effect. The number of biological agents that can be widely-disseminated is not large and with the current heightened security measures the most probable means of widespread dissemination (release from an aircraft) is unlikely to be successful. If the "weapon" has only local effect, and we can identify it early in the course of infection then our medical defenses can be effective. If we posit that the agent is highly infectious and thus has the potential to spread through the population then there will be nothing to stop it from reaching the perpetrator. Our bioterrorist, and/or his sponsor is now facing his own weapon— a thought that will probably ensure that such a release is highly unlikely. (The phenomenon of self-attack has at least one historical precedent. During World War One the German forces found themselves being "gassed" by the very weapons that they had earlier fired at the enemy which had "returned" due to a change in the direction of the prevailing wind). The potential release of a "bioweapon" such as smallpox can thus lead to an uncontrolled infection with consequences not only for those attacked but also the attacker. Taming Mother Nature may yet be beyond the wit of even the most determined terrorist.

It is the belief of the author that we should not let ourselves be ruled by our fears, but we cannot responsibly ignore the danger or fail to take steps to meet it. If the new terrorists close the capability gap and biological weapons become part of the new warfare we must be prepared, our preparedness will contribute to decreasing the threat— uncertainty in the mind of a potential attacker as to the effect of the attack may deter them from using that weapon. If we remove all the "easy options" we make waging war through bioterrorism a means that may be too much effort for the "reward" and thus provide deterrence as a component of our armory of protective capabilities. It is not yet too late but the clock is ticking and we must act now if we are to defeat the threat from this quarter— effective action will mean effective defense— there is no time like the present!

Part II

International Seminar Proceedings on

International Terrorism and Medical Responses: U.S. Experiences Abroad, Lessons, and Policy Implications

Medical Implications of Terrorism

Robert Leitch

One of the biggest problems in fighting "terrorism" is that the definition of what constitutes a "terrorist" is not a static issue. It has been said that "one man's terrorist is another man's freedom fighter"; it is also true that a terrorist in one "life" can be a politician in the next "life". For example, thirty years almost to the day, I was a corporal paramedic serving with the UK Armed Forces in Northern Ireland. We put a cordon around a building— it was a sports bar— and we were looking for some people who were terrorists. All of a sudden the back door flew open, the guy on my left leapt forward, and with his rifle butt he hit this Irishman who was coming the other way smack in the face, and he cut him above the eye. About an hour later, I put four stitches in his head. I'm now a retired colonel living in America, and he's the Minister of Education for Northern Ireland. This is how much time changes things— one moment he's a terrorist and the next minute he's not. I shouldn't really be surprised because my father was once blown out of a back window of the King David Hotel by a guy who ended up becoming prime minister of Israel. So you know, "le plus ca change".

I am going to discuss the medical implications of terrorism. I believe that terrorism is an example of what the military calls "asymmetric warfare". I want to start by making a basic premise and that the Gulf War was the last hurrah for warfare as we knew it. Future conflicts are not likely to involve large, standing armies opposing each other on a defined battlefield. Probably the best and most precise expression I've ever heard to describe the future came from an Australian who noted that "Desert Storm offers a lesson: the last thing you'd want to do is build a big army and line it up in the desert for the allies to beat the snot out of it!" The world has changed and moved on and our enemies now look for weaknesses, and they love particularly to exploit the whole weaknesses of a contemporary society. This is the essence of asymmetric warfare, a conflict in which "America's adversaries must find ways to exploit perceived U.S. weaknesses— social, political and military". Having recognized that this is my starting point, I look at terrorism as warfare and the expression by Sun Tzu has not changed "kill one, frighten a million." Accepting that as a basic tenet of what my enemy in the future will do, it then changes entirely what I can expect in the future.

What we might expect in the future is also encapsulated in the work of Brian Jenkins and Jessica Stern. Jenkins notably wrote that:

"terrorists want a lot of people watching, not a lot of people dead"

Stern offered a very convincing perspective in her book "The Ultimate Terrorists":

"Terrorists use violence for dramatic purposes; usually to instill fear into the target population. The deliberate evocation of dread is what sets terrorism apart from simple murder or assault."

One concern that I think merits consideration is the contemporary plethora of books on terrorism. I've called the expression I think a "self-fulfilling prophecy". But, I recognize what is happening now and what may happen in the future, and how it affects how I do my business and what I teach— which is medics how to do their business.

If we accept that the future threat from terrorism to the United States is a real phenomenon, then we must consider "what are the targets of terrorism?" I believe that the three most likely targets will be:

- U.S. citizens and interests abroad

- The "homeland"

- "Cyberspace"

This paper is concerned with medical responses. So I will focus on the issues that surround the first two target populations.

Target Population I: U.S. Citizens and Interests Abroad

If we consider the vulnerability of U.S. citizens and interests abroad, there are several examples of attacks in the last decade from which lessons can be learned. These could be considered the classic terrorist targets, the first one of them being against U.S. citizens abroad. In his report on the bombing of the U.S. Embassy in Kenya, former Ambassador William Crowe wrote that:

"Just to years ago, on August 7ᵗʰ, 1998, international terrorists simultaneously bombed the American Embassies in Nairobi and Dar es Salaam, killing more that 200 people. Those catastrophic acts were unrelated to East Africa and were directed at the Americans there solely because they were deemed vulnerable. This anniversary should remind us of the danger confronting our people and our diplomacy all over the world".

Crowe also wrote that:

"As we enter the 21ˢᵗ Century nearly 10 million Americans are vacationing, living or working outside our country's borders".

It took me a long time to understand the magnitude of what he was saying— that is a huge number. That is enormous— it is the population of some Latin American countries, and these Americans are spread all over the world at a great risk. It is these people who the U.S. military will have to look after in the future, but unfortunately some who are out there will probably be my casualties.

Of course, there have been warning signs if we consider the terrorist acts of the last decade. One of the first was the bombing of the Khobar Towers in Beirut. It was dealt with in a quite spectacular fashion and resulted in quite considerable number of casualties, 19 dead and 80 injured. Another involved the previously noted attack on the U.S. Embassies in East Africa— in the case of the Nairobi bombing there was an enormous number of injured (over 1,000) and dead (213) – most of them in the building next door to the embassy itself. This was, this ought to have been, a warning for all of us. The immediate impact of these attacks was to ask the question of "where is the medical support?" In fact, in the case of the Nairobi bombing, the immediate thoughts of the Ambassador turned to the need for medical help— her initial thought was that the bombing had targeted the building next to the Embassy. The *New York Times* reported that:

"She believed that the office tower had been the target of the bomb, and her mind condensed into a thought: Get to the Embassy, that's where the medics are, that's where help is."

Then she realized that the Embassy had been targeted and that there was nobody there to take care of the injured.

"I saw the charred remains of what was once a human being. I saw the back of the building and utter destruction and I knew that no one was going to take care of me."

These two comments from the ambassador herself focused on "that's where the medics are that's where the help is". What fascinated me about this particular incident when I looked at the details— was how little planning there was in place to deal with the casualties. If we accept what Sun Tzu said, which was that "I'll kill one and frighten a million," then probably just killing a few and doing it publicly like that, you don't need a lot of dead, do you? You don't even need a lot of injured. You do it publicly, you spread it around the world, and it's all on CNN.

The counter to this is that you could argue that if you have got a reasonable medical plan in place and you can mitigate the number of casualties, you're actually mitigating the effects of the terrorist attack. If you don't have such a plan, all you do is you add to the effects of the event— because there's nothing more spectacular than watching a lot of people run around in total chaos, quite stupid, not knowing what they're doing. It adds to the totality of the terrorist event. On the other hand, if you could see somebody who at least had order and planning and was doing things properly, then it would mitigate the effects of the attack for all concerned and those watching. I think what was done in Nairobi was not done well. I know the current Surgeon General of the U.S. Air Force very well, and I know that he intends for the USAF to do it better the next time. He will have the ability, when it happens, to deploy quickly Air Force resources around the world. One estimate is that USAF medical services can be "on-site" within 6-8 hours. The thing that bothers me is the figure "six to eight hours," because what will happen until then?

Those people who know about casualty treatment often state say there is a limited window of opportunity during which time you can probably save a person's life. I have to tell you, it's well within the six to eight hours. So what can be done between now and the time the "cavalry comes flying out the sky"? The answer is, if you don't have anything in place, not a great deal. This was certainly the case in Nairobi; there was not a great deal in place— there were sterling, heroic efforts by those who were there, and what they did was truly amazing, but it certainly wasn't anywhere near good enough.

So what should be done?

Planning for Immediate Response

In a previous article, I wrote a list of how I would have responded to the medical needs of U.S. citizens abroad given the increased threat from terrorist activity now and into the future.

The key elements are outlined in Figures 1-3.

Figure 1
Planning for Immediate Response

a. Good first aid training for all personnel at risk, not ATLS, unsuitable to austere environments.
b. Detailed medical Plan for first response personal: rapidly establish control in disaster area: triage and treatment: communicate with the next level of responders.
c. First aid equipment immediately available. Deployed as the Navy does in large ships.

The first response was to instigate a program that provided good first aid training for everyone. You know almost certainly that, following a bioterrorist act involving for example anthrax; the first person who is going to get anthrax will be the medic. If they are not the first infected, he or she will be paralyzed with fear, possibly blinded in one eye, not able to find their medical kit, and goodness knows what else. The immediate response is something you should be able to do yourself. It's every individual's ability to look after themselves. This first point and the allied issue of the availability of first aid equipment, certainly isn't at all concerned with advanced trauma, life support training, and the other advanced medical things that one would have to have around the place to implement them— mainly because they don't work. Not in the environment in which you need them. For example, when you're onboard a ship, there are first aid kits all over the ship and everybody knows where they are, so that if you get sealed off, you know there's one near you and you can begin that immediate response. Given the current status of possible vulnerability in a building like an embassy, you should know exactly where the first aid kits are, and everybody should be able to go and grab them.

Figure 2
Planning for Immediate Response

a. Detailed plan to evacuate casualities to initial life and limb-saving care. Local resources? Private contract in some locations.
b. Detailed plan to provide quality definitive care—may require private contract support of MOU with other nations. (Beirut bombing dealt with by the British military hospital Cyprus. Why not Israel?)

Another requirement is to have a detailed plan to evacuate casualties to somewhere safe— preferably a hospital that can do life- and limb-saving treatment. It may be the case that in many parts of the world this is a private contract with a local capability and a detailed plan to supply definitive care after that— it really does not matter what the plan encompasses just that it exists and is workable when needed. For example, one of the most interesting things about the Beirut bombing was they shifted the casualties to a British military hospital in Cyprus. As a former UK military officer I can tell you, the British military hospital in Cyprus was at that time, and still is, a cottage hospital - a tiny little place with not a great deal going on and a little bit of a problem because there was no plan in place. In contrast, no more than ten or fifteen minutes from the site of the explosion is a major hospital in Israel that is the foremost trauma center in the world. With the combined factors of the evacuation time and the lack of preparation at the site where they were hospitalized, the patients did not receive the best possible treatment and care. What is clear from all of the above is that there needs to be a plan that accounts for the medical consequences of terrorist attacks.

Figure 3
Planning for Immediate Response

a. Plan to deal with the collateral casualties—probably involve national or international disaster relief agencies.
b. Media relations and casualty notification plan will be key to morale of staff and relatives and to mitigating the terrorist aims.

The medical support does not have to be under your own personal control— it can be contracted for with another country. For example we can consider the medical response following the terrorist bombing of the USS Cole. In this instance, if there had been a contract with the French in Djibouti, we would have been quicker treating the casualties. As it was, ultimately the French dealt with them, but there was a time gap during which negotiations were undertaken to allow for evacuation and treatment. Nobody is asking to put huge resources on the ground. But what we need is a plan. A plan that is practiced carefully and everybody knows what you're supposed to do.

Target Population 2: The "Homeland"

Modern societies are very vulnerable to terrorist attacks, particularly those whose populations concentrate in cities and rely on high technology to sustain them. The United States is the archetypal high-tech society. That vulnerability is inherent in the way that we in the United States live and work. Three of the key attributes are shown in Figure 4.

Figure 4
Vulnerabilities

*   Ubanization—fragility of the modern city
*   Communication in the "Global Village"
*   Travel and population movement

In this context conventional explosives are hugely, hugely effective. Such weapons will likely remain the first choice of terrorists who are targeting the "homeland". We must however, be aware that the trend in the future will be towards even bigger and bigger incidents. In fact there are some experts that have postulated the rise of "extreme terrorism" and I find myself agreeing with their premise that future "extreme terrorists" will:

"Attack against a target without attempting to limit the damage or casualties— a potential goal of killing a million and frightening the world."

Figure 5 seeks to put in context the type of weapon that terrorists may now be considering. What is clear is that it is likely that this is this sort of thing that we can expect in the future. Why? Because of the inherent vulnerabilities in the way we now live.

Figure 5
Extreme Terrorist's Armory

- Industrial toxins
- Archetypal chemical warfare agents
- "Homemade nuclear bomb"
- Military grade nuclear weapon
- Commonly occurring microbes
- Rare and deadly microbes
- Novel microbes

If however we try and put the threat from extreme terrorism in perspective it is clear that it can be characterized as— low probability but with high consequence.

There is a plethora of terms for the possible armory of the "future extreme terrorist." They include weapons of mass destruction (WMD) and NBC weapons (nuclear, biological and chemical) and "Chem-Bio" threats. One problem with the "new lexicon" is the overuse of certain terms. Michael Olsterholm, in his book *Living Terrors*, makes the point in his statement about inability to think around certain terms.

> "*The overuse of the term 'weapons of mass destruction or WMD' has done a great deal to stunt the necessary attention to the looming threat of biological terrorism.*"

Personally, I have a pathological dislike of the term "Chem-Bio". Why? Because it promotes a fundamental mistake. It presupposes, and actually makes you think, that these are two similar systems, similar weapons that can be dealt with together and they simply cannot. In Figure 6 I have made an attempt to try and define the difference between the two of them.

Figure 6

Nuclear and Chemical weapons have a sudden and catastrophic effect on the target; similar to conventional explosives. The response required is rapid.

Biological weapons have a more insidious effect and require a more complex response system.

You can see how nuclear and chemical weapons have a sudden catastrophic effect versus the insidious nature of the biological weapon. Lumping all three weapons together exacerbates the situation, because not only does it cause us a problem in our thinking but in our training and resources, as well. The reality of the situation is that people who spend their lives dealing in chemical weapons and hazardous toxic chemicals do not easily understand the difference when it comes to a live agent. When we speak of biological agents we are speaking about live organisms. It is what certain people have termed "a deliberate epidemic" and the response to this type of attack will require significant lead action by medically qualified personnel.

If we expect the threat to increase, it is incumbent on us to consider how best to get qualified personnel integrated into our plans and responses to the threat. Bio-terrorism is first and foremost a public health issue. It must be confronted with intelligence, prediction, tracking, and all of the standard components of public health management and epidemiology not by rushing around the place "spraying people down" or being a hero— it is a careful, methodical science. The ability to deal with bioterrorism will require a new coordinated approach. The former Secretary of the Navy, Richard Danzig, put it very well:

"Only through a new union of our public health, police and military resources, can we hope to deal with this dangerous threat."

I believe that this type of thinking should underpin all of our academic thinking nowadays.

One problem that is raised by considering the works of military experts like Danzig is that of what one of my contemporaries calls "sloppy thinking". Much of what the military thinks about, in particular in terms of so-called weapons of mass destruction, derives from old military thinking. We have a tendency to still think in terms of the Cold War, even though some have said that we should have all changed after Operation Desert Storm. The Cold War is not what this is all about anymore— the world has changed, but we're stuck with this old military thinking. It is certain that with the emerging threats from terrorism and the potential for "extreme terrorism," we must change that thinking and change it fast— we must adapt to survive.

One example of how future terrorism may look is provided by the attack the Aum Shinrikyo Cult made on the Tokyo Subway System in March of 1995. Most of the contemporary thinking comes from this particular incident. The attack using Sarin gas was not very well executed but resulted in 12 fatalities, 5,500 injuries and a casualty rate amongst the "first-responders" that reached 10%. I believe that this is what the future of terrorism is really about.

Apart from the casualties the other lesson from the "cult" attack was that the use of any of the "WMD" not only causes physical trauma but that there is also a psychological issue. As Danzig pointed out:

"Panic in and of itself is becoming the new terrorist tool."

Increasingly we will be facing enemies who have taken the time to understand our fears, our motivations, and us. If you have never read the mini manual of the Urban Guerilla Warfare by Carlos Marighella, you should— the guerilla in this book got it totally and completely wrong and somebody shot him in 1970 in Brazil. His ideas were flawed except for one. He understood the concept of the strategy of "terrorist militarization". In this activity the terrorist seeks to frighten the living daylights out of people and they overreact. If you want to see it in action, remember what happened when a potential terrorist crossed the United States border close to Seattle just before the Millennium celebrations, and in response they closed the "party" down. That's militarization. When the threat from terrorism makes life so difficult that you begin to lose faith, and you're so prepared to be scared, bombed, frightened, scalded that you wait for it rather than planning to beat it, it becomes a self-fulfilling prophecy.

So the question is when will we all be allowed to set up effective planning and determine how we can react to the next surprise? I am not certain when that will be, but what I can predict is that based on the immediate past history, whatever happens next will be a surprise, one that we must start planning for if we are to effectively respond.

Medical Intelligence, Modeling, and Simulation

Howard R. Champion, M.D.

In this paper I'm going to focus on what I believe is a neglected aspect of counter terrorism, which is the medical response; and in particular I am going to discuss some of the models and simulation tools that are currently related to bomb injuries. As many people are well aware, the "chem-bio" and nuclear aspect of things are having billions of dollars thrown at them, and I believe that all that effort will bring forth something very useful to us all eventually. Not withstanding that, there remains a significant risk with the simple bomb that will blow up Americans either here or abroad; and I do not believe that we have done all we can to prepare ourselves adequately for the medical consequences of simple bombs in urban areas. What I want to do is to take things down to a finer grain with respect to the medical response. My background is in trauma surgery. I have worked in the Washington, D.C., area for many years, and in the early years, I was chairman of the Coordinating Committee for the Metropolitan Regional Council of Governments. This, of course, was just a few months before the Air Florida jet crashed into the Potomac River, and we had a magnificent display of completely uncoordinated response to mass casualties. People were still coming with ambulances from West Virginia two or three days later, and the response in the D.C. metropolitan area was absolutely catastrophic despite the fact we had predicted the same. However, we did use that event to coordinate the multiple jurisdictions and resources to develop a master plan for mass casualty response, a plan which is still in play today. In this country, we're used to a certain level of emergency medical systems (EMS) response which was first developed in the early 1970s. As a result of that, that we have certain expectations concerning EMS, which we cannot translate abroad when we go to many countries. My life as a trauma surgeon has taken me to many parts of the world, and I have helped to develop trauma systems in many countries; and let me say that the expectations that we have here are completely unfulfillable in certain areas.

So what I want to outline are the issues of risk assessment for terrorist events and linking that to the medical response assessment (not, oxymoronically, named medical intelligence outside the United States) and suggest where we should be going with respect to some of these issues.

A lot of money is going into assessment of embassies and military bases outside the United States in terms of looking at structure, perimeter, and the safety of that particular environment, i.e., preventing the event occurring. This is what in medical parlance we call primary prevention. The second aspect of prevention is mitigating the event once the event has occurred. The final aspect, so-called tertiary prevention, is treating the consequences of the event. The important element of security is interfaced between primary and secondary and between secondary and tertiary prevention. Currently we cannot provide adequate preparation for tertiary prevention, especially outside the United States, unless we have assessed the risk in greater detail than we have managed to do pretty much anywhere at the present time.

Given this status, the damage, the risk estimation, and the contingency planning are what I'm trying to vector our thoughts towards at the present time. This is summarized in Figures 1 and 2.

Figure I
Risk Assessment

√   Intelligence
√   Facility Evaluation
    —   Structure
    —   Perimeter Security
√   Damage Estimation from Event
√   Contingency Planning

Figure 2

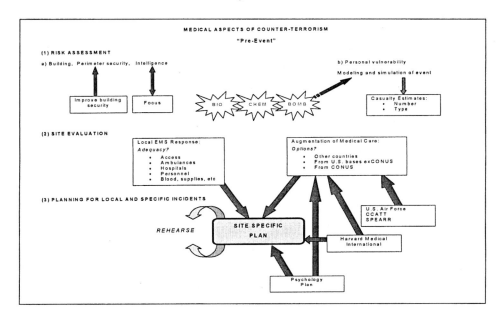

Pre-event, we certainly need the primary prevention components, which will look at the building, limited security, intelligence, i.e., whether the events will occur. Once the event has occurred, there's going to be a substantial risk to personnel. It is the estimation of the number and types of injuries, and the consequences that should flow from the event occurring that I want to focus on. That means evaluation of the local emergency medical system and comparing it against some standard. For example, access to care, ambulances, hospitals, personnel, blood supplies, et cetera: Are they going to be adequate for the consequences of the event? And how do we augment the capabilities as we had to do in a fairly unplanned fashion in Kenya and Somalia a couple of years ago?

So what we're going to focus on is that site-specific plan which involves measurements of the effect of the bomb and the measurements of the response in a specific geographic area. We know that this is going to be very, very geographic-dependent. It's going to be different in Bogota, as it is in Jakarta. The gold standard that we've entered into with respect to this is London, because it had so much practice over the years and is actually getting quite good at it.

Figure 3
Medical Risk Assessment

√ Medical Effects of Event
√ Number and Types of Injury
√ Health Care Facilities Resources
√ Medical Resource Needs
√ Assess/Egress
√ Psychologic Impact

What we're talking about in terms of medical risk assessment (Figure 3) is the effects of the event on the body. I've had a lot of research funding from the federal government over the years to estimate the effects of car crashes and bullets on the human body. My little niche of academic expertise is really the consequences of anatomic rearrangement and the time to death, and the probability of death, associated with those rearrangements. At the present time we are remodeling the effects of explosive forces on the body and we'll get into a little bit more detail on that. But essentially what we're looking at is a probability estimate of the number and types of injuries in specific buildings at specific times so that the actual dose of insult to the emergency health-care system can be estimated. Then we need to look at the health-care facilities and see whether they're able to respond in a timely fashion and provide anything like the care that we would expect in this country and that level of care we would like to think that our friends and relatives and representatives outside the United States are going to get when this event occurs. But these injuries are going to occur no matter what you do for primary and secondary prevention of the event. The event will occur from time to time and in times unexpected. Then there will be an estimation of medical resource needs, the access/egress and the psychological impact. Because that can severely impact the ability to respond even when the resources are quite adequate. Crowds of people flowing in one direction or another, people not coming into work at the medical facilities because they fear damage to themselves and want to stay at home looking after their relatives, are all factors that actually play into the ability of a specific city or environment to respond.

Figure 4
Modeling of Event

√ Blast Overpressure
√ Burn
√ Glass and Flying Debris
√ Whole Body Translation
-- Projectile

--	Fall
√	Crush

Then we have the exercise of modeling the event itself (Figure 4) (and again this might seem to be simple straightforward stuff but let me tell you when we engaged in this two or three years ago, we found that some of the modeling criteria for bomb blast injury dated back to the Civil War and had not been updated). In this undertaking we have entered into a fairly complex activity involving a number of folks in various agencies across this country and in the United Kingdom to set about modeling these causes of injury and/or death in somebody who is exposed to a bomb. The results are summarized in Figure 5.

Figure 5
Bomb Effect Modeling

√ Risk of Influence
√ Risk of Injury
√ Severity of Injury
√ Time Sequenced
√ Building and Bomb Specific
√ Based on Probable Location of People and Mass of Body Parts and Projectiles

---

You can die from blast over-pressure but in actual fact that's not very common in an event with a bomb. You've got to be standing fairly close to it and, as I've been shown for the terrorist activity in Northern Ireland, for instance, you can be standing in one spot and live and the person standing next to you could be dead depending on which way you're facing. And somebody standing 15 feet away from the bomb and from you, because of the over-pressure effect on a building, can be killed. So it is quite complex to model blast over-pressure and it is not, under most circumstance, a significant cause of bomb death. Burns can be a cause of death, but again that's not too common with bombs and buildings. Glass and flying debris is the third cause of injury–for example in a bombed building, shards of glass are produced and it's important to know about those because it's something that secondary prevention can really have some impact on and it's something that can be done quite easily. You can change the windows and put plastic in them so that the fragments don't fly. Small glass injuries superficially don't usually do much harm, but once you cut a significant vessel they can damage you quite seriously. As, of course, can flying debris, "flying computers," and those sorts of things that can damage you quite significantly. Then we have an event called whole body translation. That is a term used when you become the projectile. Your whole body is translated, and you translate yourself at a certain velocity to the wall and that can do you certain amount of damage. The other form of whole body translation is when the building collapses and you fall. From a certain height, you can damage yourself quite significantly, as well. And, of course, you can see these things happen sequentially. So if you survive the blast over-pressure and the effects of the burn, and you've ducked the flying glass and the flying equipment, then the floor might fall out from under you, and you fall down four stories and you might survive that. But then a chunk of concrete comes flying down from the tenth floor and that can do you in. So it's very important that in this sort of model these sequential effects are thought through. We know, for example that the L_{50} (level of trauma at which only 50% survive) is about five stories if you're falling. But if you survive such a fall, a flying chunk of concrete might still conclude things in a fairly definitive fashion. So we're modeling these effects now, and we have the ability to tailor it to a specific building. For instance, the American Embassy in London has 600 people in it at 10 o'clock in the morning. If you put a 500-pound bomb outside this particular corridor, what are going to be the effects? Currently, we can use specific software and say these are going to be the effects. You're going to X-number of people dead, Y-number of people with severe injuries, 50 people with no injuries, and a crowd of a 1,000 people milling around so you can't get the ambulances in and out. So these effects need to be calculated and brought into the system on some level of detail.

If we're going to pretend that we're prepared for these events, in, say, Jakarta or Bogota or some of the other places where they might actually occur, we can use this type of model. The "body effects models" give us a risk assessment of the influence of specific type of etiology for the injury to specific individuals, i.e., the risk of injury, the severity of injury and the time sequence. Moreover, it can be modeled at a level that is building and bomb-specific. For example it could be based on the probable location at a set time of the day—let's say when there are 500 people lining up for visas to come to the United States, a scenario that could significantly add to the effect of a bomb if it's timed well. So this type of model, based on known data can be put into a simulation.

If we take the model, we can incorporate the architectural structure of a given building and simulate the effects based on the type of bomb, the size of the bomb, the number of people et cetera. For example, we can simulate people in this particular room, maybe the ambassador is having a meeting here, maybe the communications are blown out, maybe the egress of a certain building, the stairwell is collapsed, and so on and so forth. The output from this type of modeling may include: number of casualties, types of injuries, severity of injury, time sensitivity etc.

It's going to be possible to model these things and simulate them quite effectively to provide the basic tool for planning. So the output of this 21st century modeling and simulation of bombs is something that I believe is a very important underpinning capability for looking at some of the medical consequences of likely terrorist events. The final thing that these types of model should provide is the time sensitivity. If you're going to die from injury, there's only two or three ways you'd die. You may die from central nervous system injury like bad brain injury, but brain injury is, of course, the cause of about 40 to 50 percent of deaths from traumatic shock. The other cause of death, which is very time sensitive, is bleeding to death. Depending upon the amount of damage, it can take you three or four, five hours to bleed to death, and sometimes you do this in a fairly conscious state. If you look at combat injuries, for instance, one of the combatants in Mogadishu was hit in the groin with a bullet. Now, this type of injury would be survivable at any large city trauma center in the United States-you get to the hospital, you have it fixed. In Mogadishu, it took that injured man two and a half hours to bleed to death because they couldn't get to him. That sort of thing can happen, and does happen, with bomb blast injuries (Figure 6).

Figure 6
Time Sensitivity of Injury/Burn

Instant Death — Major Rearrangement
Early Death < 4 Hrs.
From Bleeding to Death
Head Injury
Major Burn — Insult Doubles @ 4 Hrs.
Multible Open Fractures/Crush Injuries — 6-8 Hrs.

This is why we're particularly interested in looking at the time sensitivity of an event and the number of time-sensitive issues that come into play in a specific model or simulation. Because some of the responses in certain cities are not up to our expectations or desires, we know the severity of the output of these programs in terms of modeling and simulation of the effects on individuals.

When developing the simulation certain questions are essential (Figure 7). The sort of simulation question might be "How many operating rooms are going to be available in Tel Aviv for casualties?" In Tel Aviv I can tell you that number because the Israelis have got their act together. But I can take you to most other cities in the world, and the number of operating rooms available on a Saturday afternoon or a Friday during rush hour could quickly be exhausted.

Figure 7
Emergency Care System Evaluation

√   Emergency Ambulance Service
    --   Public
    --   Private
    --   Mobilization
    --   Level of care
√   Major Event / Mass Casualty Plan
    --   Role of security and EMS
    --   Rehearsal
    --   Update
    --   Appropriate for U.S. persons
    --   Triage rules ???
    --   Relationship with Security Forces

It's very easy to exhaust the resources of any big, busy capable urban center with a number of injuries like this. We saw it. We've seen it in a number of instances, but if you put a 100 "burns" patients into any city anywhere in the world it's going to stretch those resources. Another example might be if you have a train wreck, as they seem to be having a habit of in the United Kingdom, we know that they can treat them in London. They seem to have just such a disaster every year or so in and around London and no real surprise they're actually getting quite good at it. They can even move quite large numbers of people because they practice every year but not so many of the very, very critical ones. These critically injured ones are the ones that in certain cities are just going to die. In the United States they'll probably survive because we can get them in quickly, and in Washington D.C. we can get these figured out. But in certain cities in the world, they're just going to die because of lack of medical resources. Even if there are some capabilities, they're not necessarily going to match that person's needs in a timely fashion. We want to know about that and see if we can do anything about it. If there's a high risk, a threat, we can mobilize our capabilities quite quickly. For instance the United States Air Force Surgeon General (General Carlton) can get his equipment overseas very quickly in four to six hours.

If it was pre-positioned the day before the high-risk circumstances, you might save a number of lives, excluding of course the dead and very dead; so these are issues that make injury time sensitive. Of course, we will see instant death, but that is not very common unless it's a major crush. For example, that does occur with building collapses, and we certainly saw quite a few of them. The early death cases, those that occur in the first four hours post event are from bleeding, head injury and major burns. We know that if you don't get to adequate care system in four hours, you're doubling the insult. Now, people under 50 don't die of 50-percent burns any longer, but if you wait 12 hours to treat a 45-year-old, he's going to have a certain risk of death and we've programmed that into the results. We also know that multiple fractures and crush injuries are also important because crushed muscles causes renal failure over a number of hours.

With the injury model in place, we then have to look at the response in that particular city (Figure 8).

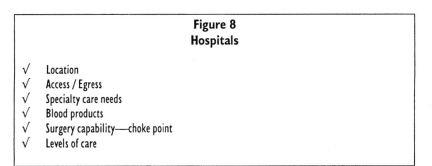

Figure 8
Hospitals

√   Location
√   Access / Egress
√   Specialty care needs
√   Blood products
√   Surgery capability—choke point
√   Levels of care

What are the capabilities in the specific city to respond to an incident? How many big hospitals are located in the city? How many intensive care beds are available? What is the ambulance service like? Do the ambulances work like an American city where you dial 911 and they take you to certain hospitals or are they going to go to a private hospital? There are certain hospitals, in for instance, Quito, Ecuador, where I have seen the emergency department with a chain across the door so that the people can't get in unless they are screened first for insurance or some ability to pay. We must, therefore, be aware that there are impediments to access to care in certain cities around the planet which don't exist here in the United States. What is more, we can't really imagine that somebody's door to an emergency treatment room has a lock. And so you have to figure out that if you've got to get this person into an emergency department and you take him or her to a private clinic down the road then you're not going to get the care that you need as quickly as possible. But these things can occur when the system is not at the level of our expectations. Another consideration is the transportation of injured persons-in many countries the ambulance services are hospital-specific. What is more, agencies like the military have their own capabilities. How do you fit into those? What pre-arrangements have got to be made? Indeed, can you make arrangements before an event occurs? So that, if you have a major event in, for example, the British Embassy at such and such a time, do you to go to this hospital versus that hospital, and is it possible to rehearse the plan? What is clear is that you've got to get into a tertiary care capability as quickly as possible, including, if necessary, the ability to mobilize the private resources in a specific location.

The relative roles of security and emergency medical systems following an incident are very important because in most cases where a criminal act is suspected, the issue of security takes over. I have worked for a number of years with the FBI— specifically the hostage rescue team— and those guys come and take over, and that's a good thing. They are protecting secondary events occurring and so forth, but they need to have been taught beforehand so that their plans interdigitate with the emergency medical teams. Accordingly, the security needs and the emergency medical needs have been the subject of communication prior to the event and are the subject of coordination at the time of the event, thus ensuring that the actions of the respective teams are not a big surprise to everybody. Where? Which hospitals do people go to? Minor wounded should not displace seriously injured et cetera, et cetera. This is not a simple thing. Triage is important in the evaluation of an emergency care response to a major event or a mass casualty event, and effective triage of the patients is an absolute prerequisite to the emergency care response taking place smoothly and effectively. If it doesn't occur in an effective manner you're relying on serendipity, and serendipity in the time of disaster is courting disaster. People die because of these things not having taken place, and at the time of the event, will die unless they do take place. So hospital access, egress, blood products, surgeon capabilities, et cetera, et cetera are critical factors in determining the outcome of an event for the injured patients.

Figure 9
Summary Grade

Level 1: Local response at highest level possible. Specific suggestions for sustaining optimum response are made.

Level 2: Deficiencies exist, but improvements can be made to optimize the ability to respond to terrorist incidence in the local environment. The deficiencies exist either intrinsic and extrinsic to a base which can be substantially resolved locally.

Level 3: Substantial deficiencies exist. Non-local resources will be required to ensure safety of U.S. Embassy personnel. This might require early evacuation of personnel, augmenting blood supply, etc.

Level 4: Environment is substantially adverse to safety and a definitive plan for external resourcing should be in place and ready.

Based on this model, we can assess the capability at a specific location, and summary grades can be given to each environment (Figures 9 and 10). The local responses need to be at the highest level possible. Local and specific suggestions for sustaining this response in a major or mass casualty event can be made in the planning component of things. Specifically, I have the embassy staff talk to the emergency medical services teams. As stated previously the gold standard we have for this is London and for a good reason–while local deficiencies exist, they can be improved intrinsic to that particular environment. Unfortunately for the majority of the world substantial deficiencies exist, and this means that additional plans have to be put into play. Specific resources need to be pre-deployed in high-risk areas, and arrangements have to made with friendly capabilities nearby. In fact, people might have to be moved out if the risk escalates to too high a level. We have heard mentioned locations like Cyprus, Djibouti, et cetera. We've got 25,000 individuals from the armed forces in the Middle East at the present time. We have some of the most magnificent hospitals in the world in the Middle East, and some of them have got wonderful capabilities and some of them don't have wonderful capabilities. If we have another couple of hundred people injured in the Middle East, which hospitals are they going to go to? What care resources are there? Is there a burn center? Is somebody there to look after head injury? Where is the blood supply coming from? Is somebody there able to do this, that, and the other thing? And then there exists the possibility of additional violence and adverse reaction and this has got to be incorporated into the overall risk assessment from a security point of view. I think this is very important that this risk of reaction be cranked into certain aspects of counter terrorism, and a local assessment take place wherever we have individuals at risk.

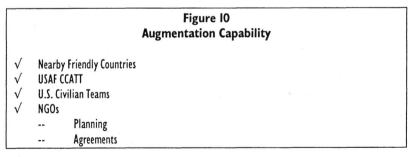

Figure 10
Augmentation Capability

√   Nearby Friendly Countries
√   USAF CCATT
√   U.S. Civilian Teams
√   NGOs
--   Planning
--   Agreements

Figure 10 shows the ways of augmenting capabilities. We have "friendly countries", and some of them have really got wonderful medical care and they're not far away. We have the United States Air Force and we have the U.S. civilian teams. In addition there are the NGOs that can do wonderful things These are all ways of augmenting and giving some confidence to those individuals that are out there doing the U.S. business that something is planned for. At the present time, there's a lot of insecurity among the citizens abroad, that they're going to get this type of care. But this all takes planning, it takes assessment, it takes agreements to be worked out up front, and they have occurred in many places.

Figure II

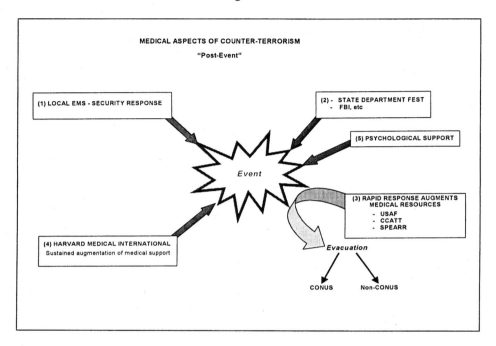

Figure 11 depicts the aspects of medical response post-event. Post-event we expect the local EMS and the security response to take place and to have the State Department have its teams to fly out there. We have psychological support, we have the United States Air Force and other people to evacuate or bring care (one or both and them), and for sustained response we'll utilize the U.S.–based civilian capabilities.

Figure I2
Summary
√ 10 Million Americans Outside U.S.
√ Many at Risk
√ Risk Estimation Possible
√ Medical Intelligence Can Be Superior
√ Risk of Death Post-Event Can Be Reduced

In summary (Figure 12) I submit that we need site-specific, or post-specific if it's military base, knowledge and a plan. The people on-site need to know that there's a plan that some higher intelligence, not mere chance, has been put in play to mitigate the effects on them as individuals when these events take place. That there has been training, that they know what will happen, and all of this will have a very beneficial effect on morale. It also speaks to the whole issue of U.S. citizens, the employees that we employ in various parts of the world, the secretaries, the janitors and so forth. They, too, are at risk, and they need to be part of this planning for aftercare when this occurs.

Once again, if we consider the gold standard, the London model, it is pretty slick. They have security agencies and New Scotland Yard (police and antiterrorism teams), the medical response team, the ambulance services, the leading trauma centers, et cetera. In London, there exists a plan, which is a detailed plan, and everybody knows about it and it's revised every year. People need to hear about it. They practice it every year and then they usually have a real incident for one reason or another. It's either the real IRA, the next version of the IRA, or a train crash, or something like that. So a mass casualty or major security event happens on a regular basis. In fact, they've actually got quite good, and that's why we've used that particular model because it's less constrained than some of the versions that we have in the United States, and, therefore, it's a good one to use. The bottom line is to develop a plan, to test it, to revise it, to retest it and so on and so forth. Earlier in this talk we mentioned Kenya: I don't want to go into the details there, but that was a seminal event. It should have alerted us all to the fact that we don't want this type of response from this type of event ever to happen again. It should not be allowed to happen. It's two years now since the unfortunate event and what has been done? The answer, very little, and what has been done has not been done very well! The recent incident with the USS Cole provided another example of a critical need. There should be a moving map that synchronizes with everywhere that a particular ship goes. It should be able to provide current, local data, such as: Where's the burn center? Where's the major trauma center? If somebody has a head injury, where are we going to get them to EMS resources? Is it Singapore? Is it Jeddah? Is it Djibouti? Every place the United States has large numbers of troops should have these tertiary care capable resources: known, available, and arrangements out there; and it shouldn't take long to evacuate the patient to that locale. We shouldn't take 12 hours to get into those capabilities. That has to be our goal. You do not want to have to perform triage when you get there, because by that time most the patients who were at risk will be dead, and most of those who at the time of evacuation are going to live will, in fact, live. The use of triage at that point in time is no way to respond to the needs of U.S. citizens engaging in important activities outside the United States.

The U.S. Air Force
Medical Response Experience

Colonel Stephen Waller, USAF

Partnerships Will Be Critical

General Carlton, the Surgeon General of the United States Air Force, is often fond of saying that one of the most important things we're going to need is partnerships to address some of these problems. With regard to terrorism, certainly that was amply illustrated with USS *Cole* evacuation, where the French bailed us out, and likewise we had a lot of help in Kenya after the embassy bombing. The key lessons from those two incidents were that the assets that we could deploy in the immediate aftermath of the incidents were insufficient— we have to have partnerships to make a lot of these things work. To illustrate that point General Carlton is also fond of saying that the last war we fought without coalition partners was actually in the 19th century with the Spanish-American War. I believe that there are two "take home" lessons in responding to international terrorism and particularly responding to explosives rather than biological or chemical events: One is the value in having small, backpack-portable teams that are very capable, that can get on the first airplane of opportunity, or check their bags (i.e., deploy with less than 70 pounds) on a commercial airliner, and be ready to go quickly. The second thing is no matter how capable we are stateside or at Landstuhl or Yokota Air Base in Japan or Okinawa, we're not going to get there quickly enough if the issue was in Australia or South Africa or other remote places around the world. We're clearly going to have to have partners. We're going to have to train with our partners. We're going to need the same doctrine, the same concepts, maybe some of the same equipment. We're going to have to understand each others' culture and each others methods, and be able to work together.

The Cold War is over. We can't be quite as simplistic as we were when we had a big monolithic enemy on the other side of the Fulga gap. We have to realize our missions are diverse and our doctrine, our philosophy if you will, has responded to that challenge. The "business" that we are engaged in within the Air Force Medical Service is shown in Figure 1.

Figure I

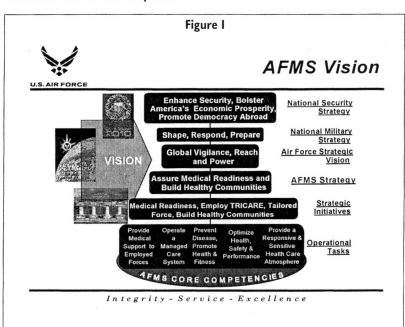

Figure 2

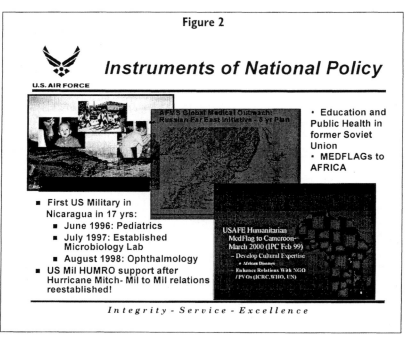

The USAF has a very complex philosophy in that we try to think strategically. We build our strategic capability from a clear understanding of all of the elements that comprise our role in the response capability of the United States military. The process requires that we build it up from the bottom-up; focusing first on our core competencies (the things we feel like we're uniquely capable of doing) up through the different directives we get from the four star generals and from the President and the Congress and build a vision. In the United States the focus changes with each administration. Under the new administration of President Bush we believe that two Committees that he is setting up within the National Security Council to address international issues will impact the work of the USAF. These are the Committees for "International Development and Humanitarian Assistance" and "Democracy, Human Relations and International Assistance". These are issues that we are thinking about in the Air Force under the new regime. Of course, the USAF have been instruments of national policy as Air Force Medics for a number of years as shown in Figure 2.

As an example, we were the first military folks into Nicaragua. We weren't perceived as being too threatening. We don't bring weapons, and as a result of that, the Nicaraguans will tell you that they were comfortable inviting our civil engineers in after hurricane Mitch to build their roads. They said if our medics hadn't been there three times and showed them that we're not all imperialist soldiers, they probably wouldn't have invited us in to help them out after the hurricane. So I think we built a relationship there using the unique medical piece that military medics can bring. This capability is enshrined in our doctrine documents. Air Force Doctrine Document #2 is shown in Figure 3.

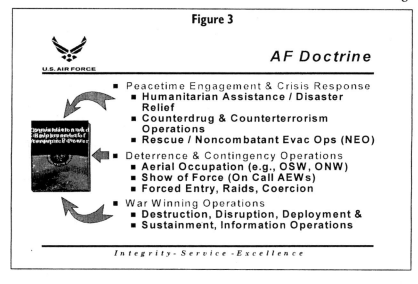

Figure 3

AF Doctrine

U.S. AIR FORCE

- Peacetime Engagement & Crisis Response
  - **Humanitarian Assistance / Disaster Relief**
  - **Counterdrug & Counterterrorism Operations**
  - **Rescue / Noncombatant Evac Ops (NEO)**
- Deterrence & Contingency Operations
  - **Aerial Occupation (e.g., OSW, ONW)**
  - **Show of Force (On Call AEWs)**
  - **Forced Entry, Raids, Coercion**
- War Winning Operations
  - **Destruction, Disruption, Deployment & Sustainment, Information Operations**

Integrity - Service - Excellence

The USAF now has a three-sided mission as shown in Figure 4. It includes war-winning operations, which has been our Cold War-era mission, but it now includes humanitarian and civic assistance as a new mission, and we have disaster response as a new mission in the Air Force medical service. Furthermore, it includes what we call "vigilance" (or "shape" activities) that is targeted at how to shape the world in a more democratic fashion.

Many of you may not know that during the 40 years of the Cold War, we had ten joint deployments. However, during the ten years since the Berlin Wall came down we've had 40! Our bosses are calling this high "operations tempo". It's a fairly accelerated deployment schedule. It taxes us to the limit, but affects our ability to project force, and we have to choose carefully what our jobs are going to be and which one we're going to decline.

In the USAF medical service on the other hand, our business is basically two-fold: medical readiness and peacetime health-care. These are outlined in Figure 5.

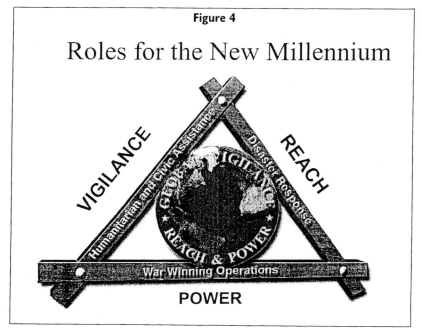

Figure 4

Roles for the New Millennium

Figure 5

U.S. AIR FORCE

The Business of the Air Force Medical Service

- **Medical Readiness**
  - **Provide optimal operational support to three major functional areas**
    - War Winning Operations
    - Humanitarian & Civic Assistance
    - Disaster Response
- **Peacetime Healthcare**
  - **Provide quality healthcare to our beneficiaries in a fiscally-sound manner**
  - **Ensure and improve health and fitness of our beneficiaries by Building Healthy Communities**

Integrity - Service - Excellence

One constant concern is that of having to draw a balance between exactly how much of our budget we apply to the peacetime health-care benefit part of our mission and the readiness part of our mission. In the context of readiness reside the three missions for projecting force and protecting our interest around the world. We have to draw a balance between exactly how much of our budget we apply to the peacetime health-care benefit part of our mission and the readiness part of our mission. We have to have diverse capability. We have to have humanitarian capability. We have to have disaster response capability and we certainly need to have war winning operations capability. In order to respond to these diverse missions, the USAF medical teams, under the guidance of General Carlton, have built a capability that can be represented as a series of concentric circles designed to show you the sphere that is our ten-person disaster response team, the SPEARR. The SPEARR is embedded within our next larger medical unit, which we call the expeditionary medical system (Figure 6). It's our smallest hospital, and then a larger hospital, which has ten beds, and then a larger hospital than that which has 25 beds. And a local commander can ask for any of these or multiples of these depending on what he or she feels the need would be.

Figure 6

U.S. AIR FORCE

Expeditionary Air Force

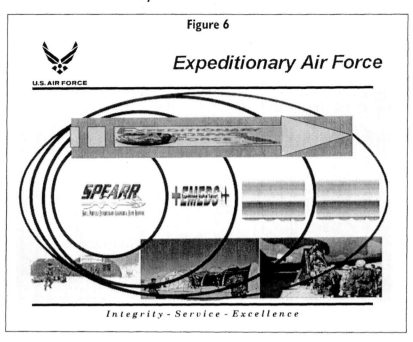

Integrity - Service - Excellence

Figure 7

U.S. AIR FORCE

Small Portable Expeditionary Aeromedical Rapid Response (SPEARR)

- Deployable within 2 hours
- Flexible -- Highly Mobile (one pallet)
  - Sling Loadable -- not tied to a forklift
- Relatively Broad Scope of Care
- Initial Disaster Medical Assessment
  - Emergency/Flight/Primary Medicine
  - Emergency Surgery (General/Orthopedic)
  - Critical Care / Evac Preparation
  - POTUS Medical Support of Choice

Integrity - Service - Excellence

The SPEARR is the Small Portable Expeditionary Aeromedical Rapid Response team. It's ten people, and comes with the trailer shown there in the picture that can be sling-loaded. It does not require a forklift, and this team can actually deploy with backpacks alone. It's been exercised up in Alaska, as you can see there at the bottom. It provides a lot of trauma capability and Mr. Clinton chose this as his preferred method to obtain medical care when he went to countries and didn't have level one trauma capability. He was in about six or eight different countries in the last couple of years of his term, including Nigeria, Vietnam, India, Pakistan, Haiti, and this team deployed with him and was on call when he was in these countries that didn't have good emergency capability. The SPEARR configuration is shown in Figure 7.

In Figure 8 you can see how it builds in capability and the types of major trauma surgeries and non-operative resuscitations it's capable of. Figure 9 configures the capability in a modular approach. that supports the "PAR" (population at risk). You can add on incrementally as your base population goes up. As the casualties from the disaster go up, or whatever scenario can be taken care of in a modular fashion. You don't have to take the whole thing at once, or you can take it all at once if you need to.

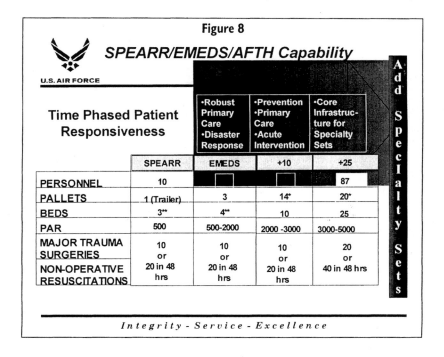

Figure 8

SPEARR/EMEDS/AFTH Capability

Time Phased Patient Responsiveness	SPEARR	•Robust Primary Care •Disaster Response EMEDS	•Prevention •Primary Care •Acute Intervention +10	•Core Infrastructure for Specialty Sets +25
PERSONNEL	10			87
PALLETS	1 (Trailer)	3	14*	20*
BEDS	3**	4**	10	25
PAR	500	500-2000	2000 -3000	3000-5000
MAJOR TRAUMA SURGERIES — NON-OPERATIVE RESUSCITATIONS	10 or 20 in 48 hrs	10 or 20 in 48 hrs	10 or 20 in 48 hrs	20 or 40 in 48 hrs

U.S. AIR FORCE

Integrity - Service - Excellence

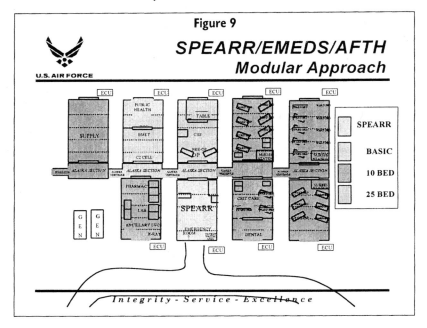

Figure 9

SPEARR/EMEDS/AFTH
Modular Approach

U.S. AIR FORCE

USAF International Partnerships

As we look at our mission and build the partnerships I was describing, we hope to be ultimately able to deploy with our partners, with our allies if you will, in different pieces. We have the same interoperable doctrine, and if we have much of the same equipment, we should be able to respond to any of the taskings indicated in Figure 10 with partners from Korea, New Zealand, or Israel, or with whomever necessary.

One new concept that we are implementing is the concept of International Health Specialists or IHS. These will comprise about 50 people who will be regionally focused. The purpose of these HIS folks is shown in Figure 11, they will be medics with speciality training that will allow them to operate effectively in the specific CINC areas of U.S. military operations. Their skills will include regional knowledge of issues of culture, language, political-military sensitivities and medical planning. We're putting them in place, and by the end of this current fiscal year, we expect to have all the major commands with a cadre of five to ten of these specialists.

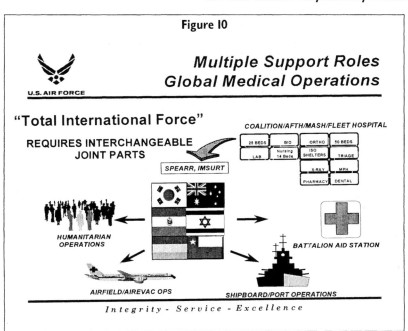

Figure 10

U.S. AIR FORCE

Multiple Support Roles
Global Medical Operations

"Total International Force"

REQUIRES INTERCHANGEABLE JOINT PARTS

SPEARR, IMSURT

COALITION/AFTH/MASH/FLEET HOSPITAL

25 BEDS	BIO	ORTHO	50 BEDS
LAB	Nursing 14 Beds	ISO SHELTERS	TRIAGE
		X-RAY	MPH
		PHARMACY	DENTAL

HUMANITARIAN OPERATIONS

BATTALION AID STATION

AIRFIELD/AIREVAC OPS

SHIPBOARD/PORT OPERATIONS

Integrity - Service - Excellence

Figure 11

U.S. AIR FORCE

IHS Purpose

- Regionally focused / regional expert / military medical resource for JFACCs / CINCs
- Focuses and facilitates the strategy of Shape, Respond, and Prepare
- Responds to HUMRO, disaster relief / small scale contingencies, and wartime contingency requirements
- Facilitates training of AFMS personnel for regional response
- Maintains and provides regional medical expertise throughout career
- Supports planning and execution of AEF strategy

Integrity - Service - Excellence

Figure 12 shows how IHS will be spread around the world. In addition, there will be a cadre of medics that will be the responsibility of the Special Operations Command.

International Congress for Military Medicine

In June 2000, at the prompting of General Carlton (Surgeon General, USAF), a resolution was passed that proposed that the "member States set up a permanent medical structure capable of intervening rapidly upon the request of a country victim of a disaster" and that member States "work out a scheme to coordinate medical and humanitarian aid such as a strategic and logistic center to unite and coordinate all energies available." The organization is going out now and looking at successful regional partnerships between military medics and bringing that back to the next meeting which will be next year. The pioneering work of the USAF in this arena is expected to be at the core of the resultant scheme. Some examples of USAF initiatives are shown in Figures 13 and 14.

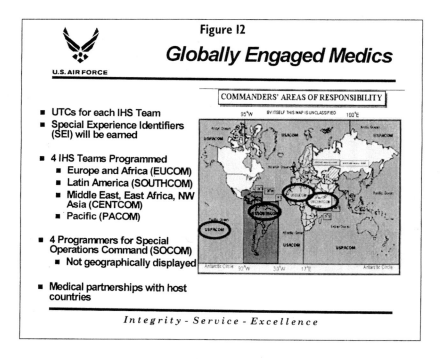

Figure 12

Globally Engaged Medics

U.S. AIR FORCE

COMMANDERS' AREAS OF RESPONSIBILITY

- UTCs for each IHS Team
- Special Experience Identifiers (SEI) will be earned

- 4 IHS Teams Programmed
  - Europe and Africa (EUCOM)
  - Latin America (SOUTHCOM)
  - Middle East, East Africa, NW Asia (CENTCOM)
  - Pacific (PACOM)

- 4 Programmers for Special Operations Command (SOCOM)
  - Not geographically displayed

- Medical partnerships with host countries

Integrity - Service - Excellence

Figure 13

Helping to Train the World

(Expanded International Military Education and Training Program, (E-IMET) MASL D309011)

- Six Day "Train-the-Trainer" Course: "Regional Disaster Response and Trauma System Management Course"

- Resource Management, Leadership, Civilian-Military Collaboration

Tailored to Regional Needs

- 3 Prototype Courses ('97-'98); First formal course Sep '99, 3 Courses 2000 (El Salvador Region, South Africa Region, Turkey)
- Building sustained leadership programs
- Over 250 coalition members trained

Figure 14

U.S. AIR FORCE

Information and Resource Exchange Opportunities

- **E-IMET Mobile Education Team**
  - **Composition:**
    - All 10 are specialists in disaster and trauma training
    - 1 pub health officer, 1 EM physician, 1 critical care trauma nurse, 1 medical resource manager/planner
    - 5 trauma surgeons & 1 surgery / critical care technician
    - Military (Tri-service & Total Force) and Civilian
  - **Skills and Characteristics**
    - Active trauma experience, TRCS/ATLS instructors
    - University affiliation; 6 instructors are affiliated with the Uniformed Services University (USU)

Integrity - Service - Excellence

One of the efforts that the USAF is most proud of is a course that we teach on trauma systems. This is the course that we have taken to El Salvador twice (Figure 15). It helps folks both with hands-on trauma skills, but also with building a system within their own country and region to respond to natural catastrophes or manmade weapons of mass destruction events. This training proved its' worth following the earthquake that occurred in that country.

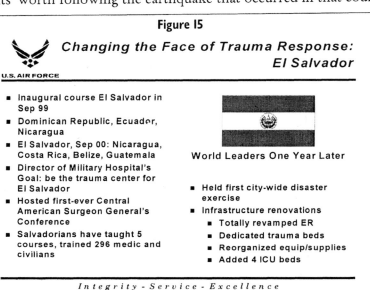

Figure 15

Changing the Face of Trauma Response: El Salvador

U.S. AIR FORCE

- Inaugural course El Salvador in Sep 99
- Dominican Republic, Ecuador, Nicaragua
- El Salvador, Sep 00: Nicaragua, Costa Rica, Belize, Guatemala
- Director of Military Hospital's Goal: be the trauma center for El Salvador
- Hosted first-ever Central American Surgeon General's Conference
- Salvadorians have taught 5 courses, trained 296 medic and civilians

World Leaders One Year Later

- Held first city-wide disaster exercise
- Infrastructure renovations
  - Totally revamped ER
  - Dedicated trauma beds
  - Reorganized equip/supplies
  - Added 4 ICU beds

Integrity - Service - Excellence

Other examples of the USAF training programs can be found in Chile, South Africa and Turkey. One very good example is that of the cooperation with Israel. Israel has fabulous capability to respond to disasters. For example, the hospital inspectors actually walk in, with no prior notice, to each hospital director in the country once a year, and hand him or her a notice that says, "in three hours your hospital has to be completely ready to respond to a mass casualty event and the event is anthrax, or the event is mustard gas." Within three hours, they shut down all the entrances to their hospital, they set up showers out in front of the hospital to clean everyone who comes and goes, and they basically completely "turn on" their disaster plan. All of the major centers are built right next to a hotel. All the guests are taken out of that hotel and those rooms all become hospital rooms, basically, to isolate, for example, smallpox or anthrax casualties. On some occasions they take over the 1,000 beds in the hotel next to their hospital. We don't have anything like that in this country, and many people would say maybe we should. Maybe that's a little bit more rigid than we want to be in this country, but we need something between what we currently have and what the Israelis put in place in a much smaller but very capable system. The basic principles are shown in Figure 16.

Figure 16

U.S. AIR FORCE

"First In" Premiere Trauma Care:
Israel

- Hadassah Hospital..Premier Trauma Center
  - Israel Trauma Course, July 00
  - Israelis guest lecturers at 59MDW
  Trauma Course
- "Light Formation:" lightweight, rapid
deployment team

  - Team of 10...comparable to USAF SPEARR
  Team
  - Responded to Turkish Earthquake
    - One of first med teams to arrive in area
    - Provided immediate emergency help
- Robust Exchanges (Trauma, SPEARR)
- Developing Partnerships / Professional Exchanges

Integrity - Service - Excellence

Figure 17

U.S. AIR FORCE

Developing Regional Response

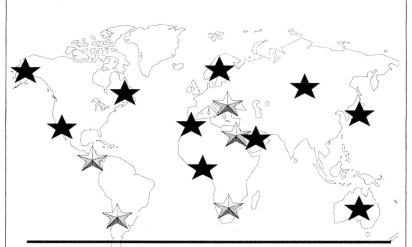

Integrity - Service - Excellence

In accordance with what has been said about an international response capability we can show the USAF regional response that we are developing (Figure 17) and the involvement of our potential partners (Figure 18).

The fact is that the world's too big for the U.S. Air Force medics to get there within the "golden hour" and resuscitate our embassy patients or our U.S. soldiers or expatriates. We're not going to make it to Singapore in six hours. We're not going to make it to South Africa within the golden hour. There's no way. So we have to build partnerships. We need to train together. We need to build doctrine together. We need to buy the same equipment, and we need to reach out to each other and share skills that are culturally and geographically appropriate. We hope to set up our SPEARR themes. However, what we're going to depend on our partners to be able to cover the whole globe.

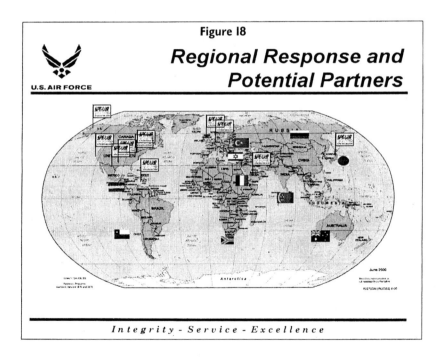

Figure 18

Regional Response and Potential Partners

So the bottom line, as shown in Figure 19 is that doctrine and strategy do drive the current changes that we're seeing in the Air Force medical system. The first change is lighter, leaner, modular teams. The second change is international partnerships and training opportunities that form the basis of an active program in the USAF to develop an effective capability to meet the potential for future demands.

U.S. AIR FORCE

Figure 19

The Bottom Line

- Doctrine and Strategy drive current changes
- Lighter, Leaner, Modular, Smaller Footprint
- International partnerships
- Training opportunities

Integrity - Service - Excellence

Sustaining the Response OCONUS

Susan Briggs, M.D.

Disasters follow no rules. No one can predict the complexity, time or location of the next disaster. Traditionally, disaster providers have held the erroneous concept that all disasters are different, especially disasters involving terrorist acts.

Thus, one of the most significant problems in disaster medical response, both nationally and internationally, has been that *we do not prepare for disasters, we respond to them.* Each disaster is viewed as a separate crisis. Past disasters have *not* been the key to successful planning for future disasters. Fortunately, organized civilian medical response to natural and technological disasters has been developing as a field of expertise during the last decade. This development has evolved as a reaction to devastating experiences with natural and man-made disasters and terrorist bombings.

It is helpful to think of disaster response as part of the food chain of *"911" emergency medical response.* When you call *"911"* in your local community, and say, "I have chest pain," you don't have to tell the emergency medical providers whether it comes from your esophagus, your stomach, or your heart to get help. When national disasters occur, *"911" disaster* is activated. Unfortunately, too often one has to identify specific disaster needs and determine which of the many governmental and non governmental organizations, often competing with each other for publicity and budgets, to call in order to get the appropriate assistance. As many of you know, there have been a large number of articles in the press criticizing the fact that, despite a significant amount of money spent on preparedness for terrorism, much of our nation is ill-prepared for the consequences of a terrorist act, especially one that involves weapons of mass destruction (WMD). This lack of preparedness is especially evident when one examines the medical response to terrorism. Internationally, there is no effective *"911" international disaster* response. Many organizations, both governmental and non-governmental, respond to international disasters. Often the response is disorganized and inappropriate, motivated more by political agendas of the organizations rather than the disaster needs of the affected population. The more complex the disaster, the more difficult it becomes to effect a coordinated response in view of political, social, and economic constraints. A coordinated response to international terrorism remains a significant challenge.

A major problem in disaster response has been our inability to identify and mobilize our disaster medical assets as a coordinated disaster response regardless of where the medical assets are located. Colonel Waller, in his portion of this seminar, emphasized the need to identify the strengths and weaknesses of our medical assets— civilian, government, and military— to meet future needs of complex disasters. Once identified, medical assets must train together to be effective in meeting the challenges of future disasters, especially acts of terrorism such as Nairobi. This, unfortunately, is a new and novel idea, both nationally and internationally. The natural disaster, Hurricane Marilyn in the U.S. Virgin Islands, typified the problems of a coordinated response from civilian, government, and military disaster groups within our own country. Civilian disaster teams of the National Disaster Medical System (NDMS), including our team from Boston, were the first medical response teams arriving in St. Thomas and rapidly became one of the few functioning medical assets on the island. Little effective coordination between civilian and military medical assets occurred. Military medical assets arrived too late and were not needed at the time. Little information was provided to disaster medical teams on the endemic diseases prevalent on the island by government organizations responsible for such dissemination. Transportation assets were disorganized with no coordinated response from departments within the government responsible for this emergency support function. Normally, each of these disaster assets is efficient when working within the organizational structure of their own group. However, the inability to change modes of operation and command structures has prevented effective coordination of these disaster assets in a complex disaster.

Another significant problem in disaster response is that disaster planning is based on the concept that all disasters are unique. They are not. Disaster planning needs to encompass the fact that all disasters have similar medical and non-medical consequences. What is different is the degree to which these consequences occur and disrupt the normal medical and non-medical infrastructure of the affected area. From a very personal point, I think the massive amount of money being spent on *"high-tech"* response elements, such as chemical protective suits, rather than training, has prevented the development of comprehensive medical planning for disasters, especially for weapons of mass destruction. There is a definable role for civilian and military specialty teams, but the first responders will be all of you in this room if your local community is affected. We cannot limit training to highly specialized groups if we are to have an effective national disaster plan against terrorism.

A further challenge in the delivery of disaster medical care is that disaster care is significantly different from the care medical providers deliver on a day-to-day basis. The key principle of disaster medical care is to do *the greatest good for the greatest number of individuals.* The objective of conventional emergency medical response is to do the *greatest good for the individual patient.* We must realign our training, both civilian and military, to meet contemporary disaster needs. Neither civilian trauma courses nor military war manuals meet these needs.

As we look to preparing our medical communities for disasters, especially terrorist acts, we need to examine critically the strengths and weaknesses of our disaster assets to develop the most effective disaster response. First, however, one must define what a complex disaster is and what are the core competencies to be included in the training of all disaster medical providers. A complex disaster is an acute situation affecting large civilian populations. It may be a blast or an explosive device with anthrax. To develop an effective response to a complex disaster involving terrorism, three questions must be examined:

(1)   What is the threat?

(2)   What are the consequences?

(3)   Are we prepared?

What Is the Threat?

Natural disasters, man-made disasters, and terrorism encompass the spectrum of possible disaster threats. Terrorism, not surprisingly, is the most challenging for medical and non medical disaster responders. No one can predict the mind of the terrorist. They are not necessarily some religious fanatics. They may be your next-door neighbors. Even Harvard has educated a terrorist, the so-called, UNABOMBER.

The potential magnitude of terrorist threats with weapons of mass destruction is unthinkable. If the World Trade Center explosion had materialized as the terrorists planned, one tower would have collapsed onto the other tower, generating 50,000 casualties. Such a magnitude of casualties would have overwhelmed our disaster system, one of the best in the world, resulting in high mortality and morbidity. International terrorist acts, particularly involving Americans, are unique challenges as the events often occur in politically unstable regions and austere environments (limited disaster response capacity—medical and non-medical).

One of the unique features of a terrorist attack, particularly involving weapons of mass destruction, is that psychogenic causalities often predominate. Terrorists don't have to kill people to achieve their goals. They just have to create a climate of fear and panic. In the sarin gas attack in Tokyo, which was a poorly executed attack in terms of actual lethality, five thousand casualties were admitted to the hospitals. Four thousand five-hundred were victims of psychological stress. Only five-hundred were suffering from the physical effects of the sarin gas. But that fact didn't matter. The hospitals and emergency medical responders were overwhelmed triaging four thousand five-hundred individuals to identify the victims needing medical care. Responding medical personnel are at extreme risk to personal injury in terrorist attacks, either because they become secondary targets for the terrorists or due to scene safety risks.

Weapons of mass destruction creating "contaminated environments" will be the greatest challenge of all. No longer will emergency medical responders be able to bring victims into hospitals, further contaminating medical facilities. Preplanning must include realistic disaster plans to treat victims of weapons of mass destruction. Disasters involving weapons of mass destruction certainly have the greatest potential to become what is known as a complex humanitarian emergency (CHE). In complex humanitarian emergencies, not only are there large numbers of casualties but the infrastructure needed to support an effective disaster response is also damaged (water, food, sanitation, security, medical facilities, communication, etc.).

Terrorist incidents are criminal events, and many crisis management agencies may participate in the response, as such incidents cross many legal jurisdictions. Medical providers, unaccustomed to working in such environments, often find it difficult to function efficiently. The number of dead victims is greater, presenting unique physical and emotional challenges for the disaster responders. In Oklahoma City, the psychological impact of the dead victims in the heart of the nation's homeland may have been just as great, or greater, as if there had been 1,000 people injured.

What Are the Consequences?

At both the national and international level, medical responders are reconfiguring our disaster response to address the ABCs of disaster medical response. Mass casualty incident (MCI) response, whether it is local, national, or international, has *four critical components,* and medical disaster plans must encompass these elements. The four critical components of disaster medical response are: *search and rescue, triage and initial stabilization, definitive care and evacuation.*

Are We Prepared?

I think the answer is no, but we're making good progress. In our nation, the National Disaster Medical System (NDMS) is our nation's disaster medical response, both nationally and internationally. Three components comprise the National Disaster Medical System and are designed to meet the last three critical medical components previously mentioned. Search and rescue teams are under the jurisdiction of FEMA and a different emergency support function. The first aspect of the NDMS system is designation of hospital beds in the event of a national or international disaster involving U.S. citizens. Unfortunately, due to changes in medical care, every hospital is operating at 100 percent capacity and limited in its ability to absorb a sudden influx of disaster victims. Even more troubling is the current shortage of critical care beds and nursing staff, core essentials in the event of a terrorist attack involving weapons of mass destruction.

The second component of the National Disaster Medical System are 52 disaster medical assistance teams (DMAT) in the United States composed of physicians, nurses, emergency medical personnel, and logistical staff. One of the pressing issues in the development of civilian, military, and governmental disaster teams is to define core competencies for disaster providers. We have traditionally used hospital-credentialing courses, such as Advanced Trauma Life Support (ATLS) and Advanced Cardiac Life Support (ACLS), which have limited applicability in many complex disasters. A challenge for the next decade will be to develop training curriculum designed for medical and non medical providers to meet the challenges of today's complex disasters, especially terrorist acts.

The third component of the NDMS System is specialty medical teams in Trauma, Burns and Pediatrics. Our newest effort, which arose out of the bombing of the embassy in Nairobi, is the International Medical Surgical Response Team (IMSuRT), sponsored jointly by the Department of State and Department of Health and Human Services, Office of Emergency Preparedness. This team, designed to cooperate with the military, represents an excellent model of partnership. It also illustrates the value of utilizing lessons learned in past disasters to build the disaster response of the future. Most importantly, it utilizes the strengths and weaknesses of disaster responders, both civilian and military, to develop the highest caliber of international disaster medical response. Currently, most of our nation's medical manpower is in the civilian sector. The military has outstanding expertise in logistics and specialized training in biological and chemical weapons of destruction. The Nairobi incident highlighted the pressing need for a coordinated military-civilian medical response to terrorism, just as previous national and man-made disasters have illustrated such a long-neglected need. The State Department asked the Office of Emergency Preparedness of the Department of Health and Human Services to expand the NDMS system to provide a rapidly deployable medical surgical team to assist in the treatment and evacuation of U.S. victims injured in international disasters, especially terrorism, and assist the host country in the care of its casualties. The NDMS Mission Statement is shown in Figure 1.

Figure I
Mission

- Triage and evaluate American civilian military casualties and classify for evacuation via USAF
- Perform (stand alone) selected surgical procedures to stabilize casualties for entry into aeromedical evacuation system
- Stage patients for evacuation by USAF AE system
- Treatment of host nation casualties

Many countries have such teams, composed of civilian medical personnel joining active military personnel in the event of a complex disaster. Probably the country that's done this the best is Israel. Within the United States two International Medical Surgical Response Teams (IMSuRT) will be established as part of the NDMS system. The East Coast Team has been established in Boston and the sponsoring hospital is Massachusetts General Hospital, one of Harvard's major teaching hospitals. I am the supervising medical officer of this team. The second team will be located on the West Coast and established over the next years. The teams will have an advance component, which can be mobilized in 6-8 hours and a main body component, which will be mobilized later as medical needs dictate. The composition of these Teams is shown in Figure 2.

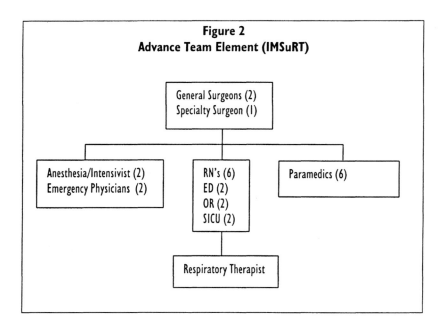

Figure 2
Advance Team Element (IMSuRT)

General Surgeons (2)
Specialty Surgeon (1)

Anesthesia/Intensivist (2)
Emergency Physicians (2)

RN's (6)
ED (2)
OR (2)
SICU (2)

Paramedics (6)

Respiratory Therapist

The IMSuRT will participate in three components of the disaster medical response. The key to the format of the teams, both from a logistics and personnel standpoint, is flexibility and mobility of disaster medical response. Search and rescue teams, two of which are available to be deployed as international assets, will be mobilized under FEMA direction and may be working with the civilian-military medical assets in certain circumstances. Triage and initial stabilization will have an advanced trauma life support level of care as outlined in Figure 3.

Figure 3
Triage and Initial Stabilization

- Advanced Trauma Life Support Level of Medical Care
- Proceed out of Teams with Advance Life Support Packs
- Deployable Rapid Assembly Shelter (Module I)

Definitive medical care has as its priority to decrease initial mortality and morbidity. The principal capabilities of the unit are shown in Figure 4. Evacuation will be by Aeromedical Evacuation System of the U.S. Air Force and other air assets as available.

Figure 4
Definitive Medical Care

- Trauma
- Burns
- Orthopedics
- Plastic Surgery
- Drash (Capacity for 2 Operative Suites)
- Operating Kits Including Amputation Kits

One of the neglected problems in disasters are injured children. When the U.S. team went to St. Thomas, our first cardiac arrest was a two-month old who required hand ventilation all the way to Puerto Rico by our pediatric specialty team members. Our IMSuRT will utilize the lessons learned from our experiences in U.S. disasters with children. Children have unique needs in all aspects of disaster medical care, including transportation.

Conclusion

The threat of international terrorism has mandated the need for partnerships in providing flexible, mobile, and the highest quality disaster medical response for U.S. citizens abroad and their host country victims in the event of an attack. As a nation, we have the medical manpower to meet the challenges of complex disasters in the next decades. We must partner, not compete, with each other.

Medical and Public Health Threats Posed by Biological Weapons

Thomas V. Inglesby, M.D.

In this paper I am going to address four key points. The first is that biological weapons are a serious and growing threat to the United States and global security. The second is to illustrate the growing power of biological science. The third is to highlight vulnerabilities of the medical public health system of the United States, especially in response to an epidemic. And lastly, I will highlight what we think are some of the key elements of a national preparedness strategy or program in the United States that might help us move forward.

There is a growing bi-partisan national security concern about biological weapons. The following quote is from the *Foreign Affairs* article by Carter, Deutch, and Zelicow: "If the device that exploded in 1992 in the World Trade Center had been a nuclear device, or a pathogen, the resulting catastrophe would have been a watershed event in U.S. history." This next quote is from the recently published report by the *United States Commission on National Security in the 21st Century*: "For many years to come, Americans will become increasingly less secure and much less secure than they now believe themselves to be. While conventional conflicts will still be possible, the most serious threat to our security may consist of unannounced attacks in American cities by sub-national groups using genetically engineered pathogens."

Why are the threats posed by bioterrorism and biological weapons growing?

There are a number of reasons. The first is simply the plausible potential destructive power of biological weapons. Work performed by the Congressional Office of Technology Assessment (1993) compared the lethality of a megaton hydrogen bomb to a serious biological weapons attack with a substantial amount of weaponized anthrax powder released from a small plane in perfect conditions to the west of Washington, D.C. The study concluded that the fatalities from the anthrax attack would be greater than those from the hydrogen bomb. As former CIA director Admiral Stansfield Turner has described, there are very few classes of weapons that even in theory could "push the nation to the point of non-recovery." Nuclear weapons and biological weapons are the two that he included on that short list of theoretical possibilities.

The second reason why the threat of biological weapons is growing is the availability of the materials and knowledge needed to make biological weapons. We know from the work performed by UNSCOM inspectors in Iraq that they found equipment that included 1,500-liter fermenter systems. The concentrated solutions that were made from these fermenters were on the order of a billion spores per milliliter. Ultimately, Iraq admitted to making 8,000 liters of concentrated anthrax solution and loading it into their munitions. Iraq admitted to making 20,000 liters of botulinum toxin, to making the most lethal known crop-killing agents, and to making camelpox— the cousin of smallpox, among other parts of its program. Compare that biofermenter to the footprint of an uranium enrichment plant such as the one in Tennessee. The nuclear plant is pretty obvious from the sky. When it was built, it required the equivalent of the entire timber production of Minnesota per year. This is a tremendous effort to make a few kilograms of plutonium. Compare this to the money and components needed to make biological weapons.

The third major reason is the concern regarding dangerous materials, cultures, scientists and knowledge. We are only now becoming fully aware of the extent of the Soviet biological weapons program that existed in the 1970s, 1980s, and 1990s. We now believe that this program has been largely dismantled, but unfortunately, there are lots of loose pieces and unaccounted scientists. The program was making on the order of 200 tons of anthrax a year at some points in some facilities, vast quantities of smallpox and other viruses in other facilities. The scope of this program was tremendous, and we are still trying to address its legacy.

The fourth reason why we should be concerned about biological weapons is the appeal of asymmetric forms of weapons, such as biological weapons. Approximately a dozen states have developed or are actively developing offensive biological weapons programs. Compared with other major weapons programs, they are not expensive. They are based on available technologies, which are used for agriculture and pharmaceutical industries. They can also be developed by non state actors. The important lesson from the Aum Shin Rikyo is not that sub state actors could not succeed in using biological weapons, but that they attempted to essentially topple the Japanese government and kill as many civilians as possible in doing so. They failed for a number of relatively unsophisticated reasons; they didn't even have senior microbiologists on their staff. I think it would be a mistake to draw a conclusion that this is an impossible technology on the basis of their failure.

The second point is the growing power of biotechnology. Nearly every day, if you read the *New York Times* or *Wall Street Journal*, you can read about the power of biotechnology, usually in the business pages. By exploring the genomes of humans and bacteria, we will soon understand far more precisely the reasons why humans get sick, why bacteria and viruses make us ill, and how they do it exactly. Eventually, we're going to identify not only the genes that do it, but the many specific proteins responsible for disease processes as well. The problem with this is that while most scientists are doing this research for the good of mankind, there is a knife-edge here where the knowledge that you have in developing a new antiviral for a nasty virus could at the same time potentially make you able to insert a gene to a viral genome and make it nastier. The life sciences have been called the science of the 21st century, with physics and chemistry the dominant sciences of the end of the 20th century. It will not be long before we can manipulate entire genomes. An example of this type of technological quandary can be seen in an article published in one of the nation's premier science journals. In essence, scientists took eight plasmids from a cloned DNA library, infected cell lines, and created great quantities of living influenza viruses. The paper published ways to recreate influenza strains which were historically very nasty or strains that never have existed before on earth. This was published without a cautionary editorial in a journal by responsible scientists and editors. I am sure their intentions were quite good, and the research makes substantial contributions to the knowledge about influenza. Unfortunately, it also now has offered a roadmap for more simply creating novel influenza in laboratories.

It is worth restating what has now become clear to many observers. The consequences of a biological weapon attack would be an epidemic. The most ominous scenario is an attack in which a biological weapon is used to cause mass casualties— without announcement, without explosion, no bomb. An epidemic would result in the community in which it was released. Depending on the incubation period of the agent, depending on the characteristics of the disease that would follow, the epidemic could look like all sorts of things. We concede that there is a range regarding the level of casualties that could be caused by a single act of bioterrorism. But we make no apologies for worrying about the mass casualty scenarios first, because the mass casualty bioweapons attack is scientifically plausible.

Let me discuss some of the characteristics of past epidemics that illustrate some of the potential implications of a modern bioweapon-induced epidemic. Epidemics are terrorizing. In Surat in 1994, on just the mention of a possible plague epidemic in the locale, 100,000 people fled the city in 12 hours just on the announced possibility of a plague epidemic. Within a day, 500,000 people had left the city. Ultimately there were less than 50 deaths, and a number of others got sick. But 500,000 persons fled a major modern city despite this being an antibiotic-treatable disease. There are some diseases that make people very nervous, very fast, and might cause public reactions which we really hadn't thought about clearly in the United States in terms of mass public response.

The second notable characteristic of epidemics is the possibility for mass casualties. The Pandemic flu of 1918 was a good example of this. The 1918 flu spread around the world in a couple of waves, but ultimately sickened 25 percent of the people of the United States and killed more than 600,000 in the United States, between 20 and 40 million worldwide. It is possible that some of the interventions that we have today could change those figures, but we are not sure that is the case. Our influenza vaccines are relatively good, and we prevent in a normal year 70 percent of influenza cases with vaccine. However, if we got the flu strain wrong or we have insufficient lead-time, and if the strain has great virulence such as the strain of 1918, the potential for mass casualties spreading quickly around the world is serious. An example of a near miss was the Hong Kong flu a few years ago, when there were only a few deaths but the world was basically watching with bated breath to see if this was a lethal and highly contagious strain. It was lethal in humans, but not easily contagious, fortunately. Ultimately, the 1918 Pandemic flu only killed two percent of the people who got sick. Despite this modest mortality for this disease (smallpox would cause 30 percent, anthrax 80-90 percent), it caused tremendous trouble around the world.

Depending on the disease, an epidemic can be contagious, person-to-person, so now your neighbor, instead of a friend helping you out of a crisis, could potentially become the person who could infect you, who you might be nervous about. Epidemics know no borders. Foot-and-mouth disease is a terrible example of this, burning carcasses, now a disease in France, a disease in Argentina. We are now restricting meat in the United States from the United Kingdom. This is not going to be over soon. The United Kingdom is trying to expand its "slaughter efforts," a quote that was on the radio this morning. Epidemics aren't over quickly. West Nile virus is still going. West Nile is a relatively non-virulent epidemic. Only a few people died, even in the first wave, but West Nile virus may be here to stay in the United States. It's expected to move further west with the bird populations this year. We know that more and more birds are being found to be able to be infected. More and more birds are dying of West Nile.

One well-known example of the biological agents is smallpox, perhaps the worst of the worst. Smallpox has killed 300 million people in the 20th century, so essentially three times more than all of the wars combined. A case history of childhood infection from the 1970s would probably read as follows: On day three of the illness the child has a little bit of rash, indistinguishable from other childhood illnesses. The rash soon becomes more serious, developing into painful pustules. The boy survives this illness, but he is going to be scarred for life. These are scars in the deep part of the skin in the dermis.

Unclassified estimates that have been published elsewhere regarding our level of smallpox vaccine places that level somewhere in the order of seven million doses. The worldwide supply of smallpox vaccine is somewhere in the order of 60 million doses, but we're not really sure how good the rest of the global vaccine supply is, and we have no agreements to get vaccines from anyone else in the event there's a worldwide crisis. So we shouldn't be anticipating that we could get ample doses of smallpox vaccine if we need it. Mortality of smallpox is estimated now to be about 30 percent. There is no treatment. The great concern is that the smallpox vaccine would run out faster than we would be able to manage a smallpox epidemic. Efforts now are being ramped up to make more smallpox vaccine at CDC.

How would our medical and public health care system respond in a fast moving, lethal and or contagious disease epidemic. Our analysis at the Center for Civilian Biodefense Studies at Johns-Hopkins University is that both the U.S. health care system and our public health infrastructure are ill-prepared to handle large-scale epidemics. For many of the diseases that we're most worried about, there are no treatments. There is no antiviral treatment for smallpox, Ebola, or Marburg virus. There are limited supplies of botulinum toxin. The number of vaccines available to treat the most concerning diseases is small, and the quantity of them, in some cases, is in relatively short supply.

Johns Hopkins is in the same state of affairs as Mass. General and other hospitals around the country. We are on ambulance bypass frequently, i.e., we can't take new patients on a regular day frequently; it's just too crowded. We share ventilators with the other hospitals in Baltimore as is the case in most cities— usually we're renting a few. Our antibiotic supply in the hospital is basically enough to treat the day's patients and maybe the next few days. There's no major supply in any hospital of extra antibiotics. Nursing shortages are expected to grow and grow for the next decade, and this represents a systemic structural problem in nursing that is not likely to fade soon. One-third of hospitals were in the red last year; a thousand hospitals have closed in the last ten years. It is generally not well-understood how little surge capacity exists in the United States for crisis. We do a great job of taking care of sick people kind of moment-by-moment, but in terms of contingencies, there is very little give in the health care system. Along those lines, we've spent a lot of time speaking to leaders of hospital associations in the hospital and hospital executives themselves. They have talked about what they're doing and what they think they should be doing to get ready for things like epidemics or crises, mass casualty events, and they essentially say, "Look, I've got a crisis that could shut my hospital down tomorrow. And it has nothing to do with low probability and high consequence events. It's essentially a routine-operating business. I'm in competition with the next hospital next door. And we're not working together. We're actually competitors." Hospital CEOs are reluctant to take on another unfunded mandate and, essentially, are waiting for some significant direction from the government in terms of incentives and leadership.

The U.S. public health system has been the neglected stepchild of modern medicine. About one dollar out of 100 health care dollars is spent on the public health system. Health departments struggle with modest-to-little resources; they're not paid well; they're staffed poorly. A lot of them don't have computers on their desks. In Milwaukee when there was a *cryptosporidium* outbreak a few years back, 400,000 people got sick, and the Health Department didn't have a fax machine. They had to borrow a fax machine from the Office of Economic Development down the hall. It is the case that if you walk around in some of the richer health departments in some of the richer states, you will notice a stunning lack of technology, not for lack of wanting it, but for lack of resources. The public health system is a misnomer. This is not a system. It's a set of component parts, which are loosely integrated and are, unfortunately, not very well-connected, certainly not electronically well-connected, and again, little resources to pull off the funds that are needed in the system.

Below are listed what we believe are the most important elements of the public health system in the event of a large-scale epidemic. First, we need to figure out that an outbreak is occurring. We don't have a lot of faith in these very high-tech artificial intelligence surveillance systems that are being funded at very high dollar costs right now. We think it's much more likely that smart people working in hospitals will realize something terrible is happening and call a health department, and say, "Can you get over here and help me figure out whether I've got anthrax, or whether this is just the flu?" In any case, no matter how the report of a suspicious disease outbreak gets there, the health department doesn't have a lot of power to investigate. They're very short on people. So even on a good day and with goodwill, it's hard for a lot of health departments to send a lot of people to figure out whether something is bad or just a distracting red herring. Recognizing the outbreak is the first challenge— and this will require interactions between the medical system and the public health system.

The second important response element is containment. I'm sure you all are familiar with the TOPOFF exercise that happened in May with Denver hosting the biological weapons component of the exercise. One of the most striking things about the TOPOFF exercise is that the epidemic continued to grow out of control, the focus was put on treating victims but, unfortunately, there was insufficient ability and attention spent on containing the epidemic. Very quickly the epidemic was moving through Denver, moving around Colorado. It didn't take a day or two into the epidemic for people to begin talking about a quarantine of people in their homes, quarantine of the city, quarantine of the state. It was not clear what level of force would be used, how people would get food and medicines, so tremendous issues regarding civil liberties, regarding logistics, regarding practical realities, did not really get tested in this exercise.

Another critical response component for public health would be the organizing of the treatment of large numbers of people, for even a very simple treatment, the logistics would be fairly staggering. Vaccination, just getting a vaccination into 1,000 or 10,000 or 100,000 arms would be a tremendous challenge. Lastly, public health would need to work with law enforcement. That's a complicated hybrid, which really hasn't had a lot of testing; but fortunately, there have been a lot of developments in good directions in the last few years on that.

The good news is government has begun to respond. Government recognizes that this is an important national security threat and a new kind of one—one that requires new sets of partnerships and possibly new organizational constructs. Agencies and organizations have spent a lot of time on chemical weapons preparedness, but I would agree entirely with what Dr. Briggs said regarding the worry that lots of attention has gone to suits and materials and not a lot to thinking about training or the essential public health or medical capacities that are needed. There has clearly been less progress and preparation for bioterrorism, but that is beginning to change. There is definitely an emerging recognition that this would result in an intentional epidemic.

We think four major components of a strategy are important at the national level. The first is, essentially, a substantial new applied Biomed R&D program. The second is preparing the health care system to respond to mass casualties following epidemics. The third is trying to foster the development of the essential public health capacities. Lastly, there are a number of things we can do in an effort to prevent this from happening in the first place. A new Biomed R&D program would attempt to harness the fantastic biological science that is now occurring in many sectors around the United States. Currently very little of it is directed to the problem of confronting the dark side of biology, and we think we can change that with the right incentives. We would need DOD and HHS, universities, and PHARMA to be engaged. If they could focus this clearly on new diagnostics, new treatments, new vaccines, make this a very applied, very specific program, answer a couple of charges that are put forth by the U.S. government, there could be major developments for the good. In terms of preparing the health care system to respond to epidemics, we first would need some basics. Let's get people to recognize nasty diseases. Essentially, try to find ways of being able to improve diagnostic times, equipment, and begin to figure out how hospitals in the event of a crisis could turn on systems and begin to work together. Right now there is no effective way of doing that. Third, as discussed above, we urgently need to shore up public health capacity around the nation. Finally, there are a number of potential prevention efforts that should be supported. The Biological Weapons Convention is in some trouble. I don't know how it's going to come out. We're worried that no matter how it comes out, that it will carry unenforceable, unverifiable commitments, but certainly nation-to-nation arms control is, we think, still important. We also need to create incentives to stop scientists from setting out to, or returning to, work on biological weapons. There is much that can and should be done to confront the problem of biological weapons.

International Terrorism and Medical Responses: The Shape of Things to Come?

Stephen Prior

The dominant role that the United States now plays in international affairs and the increased U.S. commitment of military personnel to operations outside of the continental United States (OCONUS) has made the United States a significant target for potential terrorist action. The U.S. mainland has, thankfully, remained largely free of direct action by terrorist groups or lone actors. However, this is not a reason to become in anyway complacent. The current level of vigilance that operates at points of entry to the United States has deterred most terrorists from trying to penetrate the homeland defenses; but in the future the temptation will be great. A successful terrorist strike on U.S. soil is becoming the ultimate challenge to the United States government and an increasing signal of power for terrorist groups around the world. It is imperative that we redouble our efforts to prevent such an act from occurring. As a consequence, we need to further develop our intelligence efforts that target counter-terrorism and increase our programs to develop new technologies that offer the capability to deter the putative terrorist or, if they are successful in perpetrating such a heinous crime against the homeland, to mitigate the effect of their actions. Unfortunately, our success "at-home" will increase the risk to those U.S. citizens, civilian or military, who operate outside of the United States. With the advancing "global economy" and an ever-larger political role on the world stage, there is an increasing population of U.S. citizens who will be exposed to the threat posed by terrorist actions. This requires that we review our current response capabilities and seek to strengthen them in any way possible.

In the past decade we have witnessed an increase in the targeting of both U.S. assets (facilities and equipment) and personnel overseas. The current estimate of over 10 million U.S. citizens living or working abroad represents a major vulnerability. It also creates a logistic problem in terms of U.S. support and response in the event of an incident, whether the cause is a natural disaster or as appears increasingly likely the result of terrorist action. Furthermore, the personnel are, for the most part, located in close proximity to one another and are readily identified. In fact, centralized U.S. assets such as embassies and military installations or visiting military assets, such as the USS *Cole* in Yemen, have become the principal targets for terrorists wishing to attack the United States. Most of the terrorist attacks on U.S. assets, interests, and personnel, and nearly all of their significant "successes" in the last decade, have been in the group listed above. The increasing spectrum of terrorist weaponry (both conventional and asymmetric) provides a challenge to the responder teams, requires extensive and constant education and training as well as a need to update physical protective capabilities as new technology becomes available. At present many U.S. facilities and assets overseas, particularly those in the civilian sector, lack the latest technology to combat potential terrorist acts. Some even lack suitable physical barriers that prevent terrorists from penetrating a safety zone and getting in close proximity to their targets. The recent experience with the USS *Cole* provides a good example of the lethality of conventional weapons if they can be detonated in close proximity to a target. A comprehensive review of the current technology that can be used to mitigate potential vulnerability to terrorist activity would appear to be of great value and will be discussed throughout the series of seminars that will be hosted by the National Security Health Policy Center (NSHPC) and the International Center for Terrorism Studies (ICTS) at the Potomac Institute for Policy Studies.

In a new book (*Super Terrorism*, Transnational Publishers, Inc.) that reviews the growing concern about terrorism, Drs. Alexander and Hoenig state "modern terrorism is poised to enter a new dimension–super terrorism–characterized by covert biological, chemical, radiological, or nuclear attacks to achieve mass destruction and casualties. While there is broad convergence on the possible consequences of superterrorism, there is robust disagreement on the kind of investment that should be made in preparedness and response. Should the effort be geared to correcting all vulnerabilities or to responding to a low probability/high consequence threat in a more limited way?" This is a large and complex issue that merits much discussion. This paper seeks merely to draw attention to the medical aspects of any such response and the current limitations of that response in terms of planning and policies. Furthermore, the paper seeks to characterize the differing types of response required for each possible category of terrorist event. One aspect of the medical response that this paper makes no attempt to address is the psychological intervention that will be needed to support those affected by a critical incident. In their excellent book. *Critical Incident Stress Management-CISM* (Chevron Publishing, 1999), Everly and Mitchell present a coherent treatise on the need to prepare for crisis intervention from a psychological perspective. In future seminars NSHPC will explore this complex and essential aspect of the medical response. The subject of CISM remains beyond the scope of this paper.

What is absolutely clear is that:

- The quality and timeliness of the medical response are the most important elements in determining the outcome for the victims of a terrorist event.

- Provision of the best possible medical response is thus a critical element in planning to mitigate a terrorist event.

- Medical response planning cannot be added after the event if it is to influence the outcome for the victims. It must be an integral part of the plan from the outset, it must be widely discussed and everyone who is involved should understand his or her individual roles and responsibilities.

In the first of a series of seminars that will discuss "Medical Responses to Terrorism" the NSHPC and ICTS reviewed the current status of medical response from a U.S. perspective. The proceedings, published in this volume, show that while some excellent examples of implemented planning exist, there is enormous scope for improvement. Earlier in this paper, it was noted that there is an increasing trend for the terrorist who wishes to target the United States to do so OCONUS. If this trend continues, it will be imperative that our planning and policies for dealing with the consequences include measures that engage the support of our allies overseas. In their presentations both Dr. Briggs and Col. Waller stressed the value in such outreach activities and how the availability and effective use of foreign-based medical assets can significantly improve the potential outcome for the victims of an OCONUS incident whether man-made or natural in origin. Furthermore, our current plans and policies reflect past experience and do little to predict future trends or requirements. In his excellent article, Dr. Howard Champion reveals an outline for a modeling and simulation tool that can be adapted for specific locations and scenarios of terrorist events. The reader is encouraged to read the article by Dr. Champion for more details. Building on the work of Dr. Champion, this paper provides a second tool— one that represents an attempt to show the very real differences that exist in the medical responses to various types of terrorist events.

In reviewing the four major "types" of terrorist act, there are clearly major differences in the physical medical specialties that must be employed to respond to the event. (Note: The psychological medical response, a response well-documented as CSIM [Everly & Mitchell, 1999]) may also be an immediate need but it is not considered in this simple initial model. Later models will attempt to include this response through exploration in future NSHPC seminars). Each type of event can be characterized as having a "shape" that defines the required medical response in terms of primary, secondary, or tertiary care. While no "solution" fits all the scenarios, some general patterns are discernable. The basic outline of the model is shown in Figure 1.

Figure 1

A 3-Dimensional Model of Medical Response

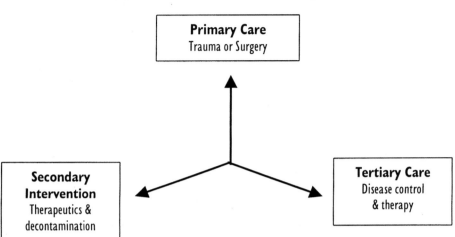

This model can be applied to the four major types of terrorist act and indicates the different patterns of medical response that will be required to meet the casualties that will result from the specific terrorism event. This is shown in Figure 2.

Figure 2

Application of the Prior 3-D Model to Terrorist Incidents

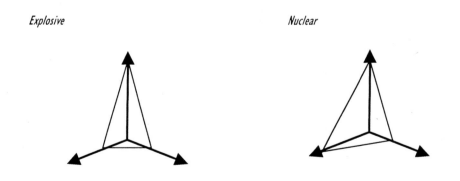

Explosive   *Nuclear*

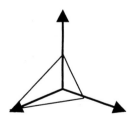

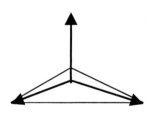

The models can also be utilized to provide some evaluation of the extent of resources that may be required. Firstly, the overall "shape" provides a clear indication of the type of medical response most likely to be required. For example, the use of an explosive device will probably lead to significant physical damage to the victims' body extremities requiring surgical intervention, whilst the explosive shock will require extensive trauma treatment of the victims. By contrast, the release of a biological agent is likely to be "silent," offering little or no injury at the point of release but requiring massive input, for example, in terms of antibiotic intervention. Secondly, if the individual axes of the model represent actual capability, based on database information from any given site/situation, the volume of the "shape" created by analyzing the characteristics of the event indicates not only the overall "shape" but also the magnitude of the required medical response.

In future seminars that will be held by NSHPC and ICTS, the use of these models and other graphic representations of the medical response to terrorism will be discussed and evaluated to determine their possible use in establishing plans and policy both in the United States and OCONUS. While acknowledging that medical response is only one component of the total crisis intervention response to a critical incident, such as an act of terrorism, it is nonetheless of crucial importance. The adequacy of our medical response, i.e., the ability to effectively implement the plans and policies developed prior to an incident, will remain a crucial determinant of the outcome of the incident. This is especially true for the victims directly affected by the event. The current lack of effective plans and policies, whether in the United States or OCONUS, delineates a vulnerability that needs to be urgently addressed and is a topic that will be a focus for the forthcoming work at the NSHPC.

In addition to our effective implementation of plans and policies the other key determinant for the outcome of a bioterrorist or biological warfare attack will be the capability of our medical teams to treat those affected. This has led us to propose a second topic that we will be discussing in follow-on seminars, i.e., the need to protect the critical personnel that may be required to respond to a bioterrorist incident. The principal concern will be the protection of critical personnel on medical response teams that are first called upon to deal with the incident. These personnel are often referred to as "first-responders" the first-responder teams will include doctors, nurses, and paramedic staff but may also include personnel responsible for ambulance or evacuation vehicles, firefighters, police, pharmacists, etc. The specific type of incident will also determine which ancillary personnel are destined to play key roles. Even though it is difficult to plan for all eventualities "some plan is better than no plan".

If a terrorist act targets a U.S.-owned asset overseas, the first U.S. responders will likely be the surviving personnel on-site. In the case of a biological attack, this will mean those individuals who have been exposed to a challenge dose below that causing infection or those personnel with preexisting protective immune responses derived from vaccination or prior exposure to the disease-causing agent. If the attack is on U.S. personnel "at-large" rather than those in a fixed asset (facility, vehicle, etc.) the first U.S. responders will likely be from the closest U.S. military asset or the embassy personnel currently residing "in-country". In either case it is imperative that the first-responders are able to access the resources and support tools that will enable them to effectively intervene to try and minimize the effects. It would appear axiomatic that the capability of overseas first-responders be properly reviewed and updated to ensure that they are well-prepared for any of the possible types of terrorist action or even natural disaster that may occur.

The best possible education and training should be provided as well as the latest technology for detection, prevention, and response to the full range of possible weapons. Although conventional weapons represent by far the greatest threat, the possibility that other weapons may be used cannot be discounted and require that they be considered a component of any review of the present and future threats. In addition, host-nation support for U.S. personnel overseas may be of critical importance in determining the outcome of an event. In some cases this capability is further hampered by cultural and language barriers that complicate the response to an event and increase the vulnerability of any victims.

In the context of the "shape" (see Figure 2 above) of the medical response to a specific incident, there is a compounding effect that is at its most obvious when the incident involves biological weapons. Following any incident, the immediate access to medical teams is finite and dependent on a number of factors including proximity to a hospital or hospitals, location in urban or rural area, time of day, etc. It may be possible within a fairly short time to access additional staff, equally those on site at the time of the incident may be all that is available. Any degradation in the capability is likely to impact the ability to treat victims and thus significantly influence the outcome of the event. Loss of medical teams, even with their sometimes limited capacity to respond, represents not only a loss of critical capability but is also extremely damaging to the morale of the survivors.

In the case of the use of an explosive device, unless the blast victims actually include the medical staff, the medical teams will be able to function for as long as medical supplies and their own energy levels can be maintained. In this case, the capacity to respond will be directly related to the numbers of medical staff and their access to appropriate resources. With nuclear and chemical weapons, there will be a need to protect the medical teams from the effects of the materials that have caused the damage. This can be achieved through the use of decontamination procedures and/or barrier nursing. The latter requires that the medical staff use physical barriers to prevent them becoming harmed by the material used to inflict damage on the initial victims. In these cases the availability of medical capacity will be determined by the factors noted above as well as the factors that relate to decontamination and barrier techniques. For example, decontamination facilities, materials, and test equipment may not be readily accessible or be available only in limited quantities. Similarly the availability of suitable shields, masks, etc. may limit the degree to which the medical staff can perform work on patients in relative safety. When consideration is given to biological weapons (BW), the situation for medical response teams is much more complex. Firstly, there exists a wide range of potential BW agents with widely different characteristics. For the purpose of example, three such "classes" of BW agent will be considered. These are shown in Table 1.

Table I

Classes and Characteristics of BW Agents

Class of BW Agent	Example(s)	Characteristics
Toxin	Botulinum toxin	Similar to chemical weapons; relatively fast-acting, non-infectious, non-transmissable. Extent of effect directly related to dose at point of exposure.
Vector-borne pathogen	Dengue fever	Infecting organism spread by vector (insect etc). Transmission from host to human requires vector. Extent of effect dependent on host/vector/victim interaction. May be controlled by destroying vector.
Contagious pathogen	Smallpox	Organism spread by human contact. Initial infection may cause widespread disease. Direct intervention in patients often required to treat disease. Difficult to control without use of patient isolation.

Figure 3
Biological Warfare Agents and Their Impact on Medical Staff Availability

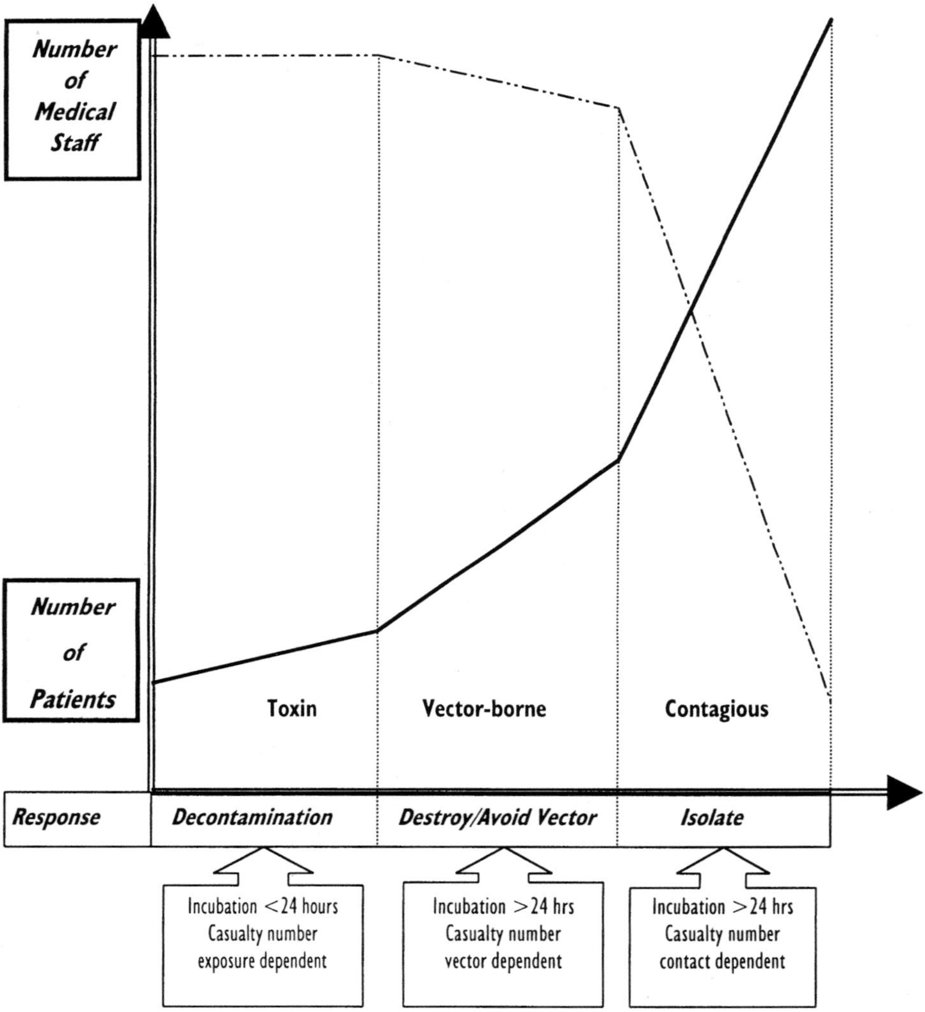

Exposure to BW agents in the form of toxins constitutes a hazard that is entirely analogous to exposure to hazardous chemicals or even some of the chemical warfare agents. The hazard is posed by inhalation, ingestion, or entry through an existing wound. There is little or no risk of entry through the skin—a significant risk with many chemical warfare agents. In the case of toxins, the immediate response will involve physical methods to control the level of contamination and medical intervention to treat the victims. At present, our options for treatment, following exposure to toxin-based BW agents, are extremely limited and involve for the most part the use of antibody-based products (polyclonal or monoclonal antisera). With vector-borne BW agents (diseases), we can intervene in an effective manner at two levels; firstly, the victims can be treated using both antibody and antimicrobial products, although as with toxins our current capability to protect against the most-probable or high-threat BW agents is again very limited. Secondly, we can interrupt the spread of the disease by destroying the vector that is responsible for its transmission. Although this action will necessarily also kill harmless, related vector species, the disruption of the host/victim cycle will greatly diminish the rate of spread and enable the patient numbers to be limited. This situation is graphically represented in Figure 3.

When consideration is given to the situation involving a contagious disease, the scenario is much more frightening. The interruption in transmission of the disease is best accomplished by isolating those already infected—although this can represent a difficult medical, moral, and ethical dilemma. Treatment may be possible but many high-threat BW agents are selected on the basis of the limitations of treatment for those exposed to the agent. Furthermore, with the increasing capacity to use molecular engineering, the particular agent may be engineered for resistance to the common forms of treatment. The major difference from the previous two examples is, however, the impact of a contagious disease on the medical teams—without adequate protection, the medical staff can rapidly become victims. This compound effect of an increasing patient population with decreasing medical staff can escalate the problems of controlling this type of putative BW attack. The overall impact could be catastrophic, or in medical terms an epidemic: Neither word adequately conveys the negative impact of such a problem and points to a real need to assess our vulnerability in terms of medical response even if the cost is significant. In the past two years, the Center for Disease Control (CDC) reported that it has begun to address some of the medical issues through the funding of the Office of Bioterrorism Preparedness and Response. This office has addressed itself to the development of a national stockpile of antibiotics and related products. But that constitutes only a small part of the overall requirement for a response. It is a good start but requires more resources if it is to address the entire spectrum of medical response issues in meaningful way.

In terms of the low probability/high consequence incident that a BW agent could represent, the ultimate cost for not planning for successful intervention and mitigation may be too high a cost for any nation. No one wishes to be alarmist, and it is clear that the probability of an terrorist incident involving BW agents is still low. But while the possibility exists and the consequences of leaving our planning at the level of the status quo remain so catastrophic, a program of review, planning, and policy implementation is not only prudent but is, in the opinion of this author, an immediate, essential requirement for the nation.

Communication: The Vital Element of Medical Response to Terrorism

Fred Cecere, M.D.

To evoke maximum terror on the part of the target group, terrorists attack unprepared targets with unexpected force. The nature, timing and location are designed to create maximum feelings of vulnerability and fear. Thus, any action, which brings aid and comfort to the victims, works counter to the terrorist's plans. First responders are trained to rush to the scene and immediately begin tending to the needs of the survivors. They arrive with equipment, sirens, people, media and sufficient noise and commotion to often render the scene chaotic and disorganized. Although the immediate effect is to lessen the fear and shock and demonstrate control of the situation, these aid workers may become targets of weapons timed to detonate coincident to their arrival.

Prior planning, realistic training, proper equipment and well-organized evacuation and supply systems are essential, but communication is vital. Without communication, proper timing of responders, for example the rapid deployment of explosive experts simultaneous with the deployment of medical teams, would not be possible. Without communication, the initial chaos could not be overcome, appropriate equipment summoned, evacuation staged and survivors rapidly moved to safe locations. Most importantly, when the unexpected occurs, e.g. a second explosion, the collapse of a structure or the sudden release of a chemical agent, a new communication requirement is created. The ability to link to a command and control center is critical. The center cannot only send needed equipment and reinforcements but can formulate tactics and strategies to deal with contingencies.

First responders on the scene almost always have a sense of not enough time, people, coordination, information and training. In a sudden act of nature, earthquake, hurricane, tornado or mudslide, these feelings can be almost overwhelming. However, only rarely does the responder feel threatened. In a terrorist event, the situation is designed to make everyone, including the responders, feel threatened and vulnerable. Information is not enough. This information must be rapidly transformed to knowledge. Thus, not only must the means of transmission be well defined, but also the content carefully selected for usefulness, appropriateness, and accuracy.

Over the next few years, new technologies will make communication easier, more reliable, and more convenient. Tools will be created that bring sophisticated technology to the aid of victims of accidents, disasters and terrorists. Communication breakthroughs will allow rivers of data to flow to and from the site. This river must be controlled or the system will be overwhelmed. Telemetry data must be sorted and ascribed appropriately to individuals. Responder's telemetric data differentiated from victims. The first information that an unexpected event has occurred may come from sudden changes in this data simultaneously from both the victims and responders.

Successful employment of these technologies will require unprecedented cooperation among commercial, academic, scientific and governmental groups and agencies. New communication and health policies may be needed to remove potential barriers and promote productive development and deployment. The National Security Health Policy Center has been created to focus the debate on how existing and new or proposed legislation and/or policies, impact the ability of the United States government to maintain national security while preventing, detecting, and responding to these emerging threats. Hopefully, through programs like this we are fulfilling this charter. Future programs are designed to further elucidate these issues of communication technologies, content, knowledge and necessary legislation and policies.

Current Status of Protection Overseas for US Citizens, Facilities and Military Assets

The seminar provided both real-world examples of current response capability (Dr. Briggs and Col. Waller) as well as examining how improved modeling and simulation may be used to implement more effective responses at the local, regional and global levels (Dr. Champion). In the context of the issues raised in the seminar the following review of the current status of a US response has been prepared.

US Government Facilities

US Embassies

The seminar speakers highlighted some of the issues that need to be addressed to establish an effective medical response for US citizens operating overseas. Many of the issues stem from the experiences of US personnel involved in the tragic bombings of the US Embassies in Nairobi, Kenya and Dar es Salaam, Tanzania that occurred in August 1998.

The report of the "Accountability Review Boards" that convened to examine those bombings included the following statements:

Executive Overview

The near simultaneous vehicular bombings of the US Embassies in Nairobi, Kenya, and Dar Es Salaam, Tanzania, on August 7, 1998, were terrorist incidents costing the lives of over 220 persons and wounding more than 4,000 others. Twelve American USG employees and family members, and 32 Kenyan and 8 Tanzanian US Government employees, were among those killed. Both chanceries withstood collapse from the bombings, but were rendered unusable, and several adjacent buildings were severely damaged or destroyed. In examining the circumstances of these two bombings, the Accountability Review Boards for Nairobi and Dar Es Salaam determined that:

1. The terrorists intended to destroy the chanceries; to kill or injure US Government employees and others in the chanceries; and to damage US prestige, morale, and diplomacy. Thus, according to P.L. 99-399, the incidents were security related.

2. The security systems and procedures for physical security at the embassies in Nairobi and Dar Es Salaam as a general matter met and, in some cases, exceeded the systems and procedures prescribed by the Department of State for posts designated at the medium or low threat levels. However, these standard requirements had not sufficiently anticipated the threat of large vehicular bomb attacks and were inadequate to protect against such attacks.

The Department of State, in fact, does not apply its security standards fully. For far too many* of its overseas facilities it implements them only "to the maximum extent feasible," applying "risk management." For example, neither the chancery in Nairobi nor in Dar Es Salaam met the Department's standard for a 100 ft. (30m) setback/standoff zone. Both were "existing office buildings" occupied before this standard was adopted; so a general exception was made. The widespread use of such exceptions worldwide with respect to setback and other non-feasible security standards reflects the reality of not having adequate funds to replace all sub-standard buildings within a short period of time. Thus in the interim before Inman buildings could be constructed, exceptions were granted. In light of the August 7 bombings, these general exceptions to the setback requirement in particular mask a dangerous level of exposure to similar attacks elsewhere.

[* Note: Passages here and elsewhere in this document marked with an asterisk (*) indicate more details can be found in the classified version of the report.]

3. The security systems and procedures relating to actions taken at Embassies Nairobi and Dar Es Salaam were, for the most part, properly implemented. In Nairobi, the suicide bomber failed in his attempt to penetrate the embassy's outer perimeter, thanks to the refusal of local guards to open the gates. In Dar Es Salaam, the suicide bomber likewise failed to penetrate the perimeter, apparently stopped by guards and blocked by an embassy water truck.

However, neither post's Emergency Action Plan (EAP) anticipated a car bomb scenario. Nor were there explicit Department requirements for dealing with such contingencies in EAP worldwide guidelines.

This lack of planning speaks to the topics raised during the seminar. There are too few plans available that are based on relevant modeling and simulation. For example, the lack of a plan considering the potential use of a vehicle-bomb is astounding. The use of vehicle bombs has long been established around the world as a means of delivery for terrorist bombs. There are countless examples of such incidents and for the USA official sources to have not planned for such an attack is doubly surprising given that both recent homeland attacks at the World Trade Center, NY and the Oklahoma bombing used vehicle mounted devices. The use of vehicles is essential for an unsophisticated bombing attack because of the amount of explosive that needs to be delivered to the chosen target. It is only when terrorists have access to high-explosive where the amount of material to be delivered becomes readily concealable. In addition the triggering of a vehicle-bomb is relatively simple involving time-delay fuses, motion sensors or electrical means of ignition. Thus providing a simple means for the less-sophisticated terrorist. More sophisticated detonators using for example timing devices are likely to be discovered during routine screening and are often readily detected— the vehicle-bomb is an effective delivery device for large bombs and a proven means of disguising the detonation device.

The Accountability Review Boards also made a series of recommendations. The relevant recommendations for crisis management are reproduced below:

Key Recommendations

Better Crisis Management Systems and Procedures

1. *Crisis management training for mass casualty and mass destruction incidents should be provided to Department of State personnel in Washington to improve Task Force operations to assure a cadre of crisis managers.*

2. *A revitalized program for on-site crisis management training at posts abroad should be funded, developed, expanded, and maintained.*

3. *The FEST should create and exercise a team and equipment package configured to assist in post blast crises involving major casualties and physical damage (while maintaining the package now deployed for differing counter terrorism missions). Such a new configuration should include personnel to assist in medical relief, public affairs, engineering and building safety.*

4. *A modern, reliable, air-refuelable FEST aircraft with enhanced seating and cargo capacity to respond to a variety of counter terrorism and emergency missions should be acquired urgently for the Department of State. Clearly defined arrangements for a backup aircraft are also needed.*

5. *The Department of State should work closely with the Department of Defense to improve procedures in mobilizing aircraft and adequate crews to provide more rapid, effective assistance in times of emergency, especially in medical evacuations resulting from mass casualty situations. The Department of State should explore as well, chartering commercial aircraft to transport personnel and equipment to emergency sites, if necessary to supplement Department of Defense aircraft.*

6. *The Department of State should ensure that all posts have emergency communications equipment, basic excavation tools, medical supplies, emergency documents, next of kin records, and other safety equipment stored at secure off-site locations in anticipation of mass destruction of embassy facilities and heavy US casualties.*

The full text can be found at

www.state.gov/www/regions/africa/board_overview.html

To their credit the Department of State did develop reactive measures that addressed some of the issues raised. These were outlined in the document reproduced below:

Department of State-Issued Guidelines August 2000

Clearly much needed to be done to improve the safety of the facilities and to enable a response to any incident to be of real value. The Department of State has the lead in such action and released the following information concerning the improvements implemented following the 1998 bombings and the report of the Accountability Review Boards.

The Department of State overseas security improvements have been implemented according to a recent publication that provides the following details:

Overseas Security Improvements

The Department has implemented many noteworthy security steps at our diplomatic missions abroad since the August 7, 1998 terrorist bombings of the U.S. Embassies in Dar Es Salaam and Nairobi. While we will not discuss specific security measures taken at specific posts, the Department has:

- *Deployed hundreds of Diplomatic Security Special Agents overseas on temporary assignment to augment security at our diplomatic missions;*

- *Enhanced the physical security at U.S. missions with additional barriers, reinforced perimeter walls, bollards, closed circuit TV cameras, video recording equipment, hardened guard booths, vehicle barriers, bomb detection equipment, shatter resistant window film, armored vehicles, access card control systems, and walk-through metal detectors, and x-ray equipment;*

- *Installed additional alarm and public address systems at embassies and consulates to alert personnel to impending emergency situations and have instituted a program for employees to "duck and cover" when the alarms are sounded.*

- *Established mandatory inspections of all vehicles entering U.S. diplomatic facilities;*

- *Worked closely with host governments to close streets or change traffic patterns in front of US missions in a number of cities;*

- *Worked closely with host governments to increase their security presence at our facilities worldwide;*

- *Continue our efforts to acquire surrounding properties to increase setback;*

- *Established surveillance detection teams at almost all of our diplomatic posts;*

- *Expanded Anti-Terrorism Assistance Training to aid foreign police in combating terrorism through such programs as surveillance detection, border security, explosive detection, crisis management, and maritime security;*

- *Enhanced training for Diplomatic Security Special Agents and Regional Security Officers to provide them additional instruction on counter-terrorism methodology, explosive ordinance recognition and disposal, chemical and biological weapons threats and defenses, and surveillance detection techniques;*

- *Created a Chemical Biological Weapons countermeasures program based upon education, training, and equipment. Worldwide surveys have been conducted to determine vulnerabilities to such attacks. Appropriate equipment has been distributed to all posts, and the Bureau of Diplomatic Security has established a comprehensive training program for security professionals and first responders.*

- *Strengthened our working relationship with the intelligence community regarding assessment, investigation, and dissemination of threat information directed at our posts abroad. Assigned additional State Department personnel to various intelligence community agencies, including the CIA Counter Terrorism Task Force, the FBI's International Terrorism Section, and various FBI Joint Terrorism Task Forces;*

- *Hired and trained 337 new Diplomatic Security special agents, security engineers, security technicians, diplomatic couriers, and civil servants;*

- *Created 140 new security officer positions abroad. By the end of FY-2000, 420 Diplomatic Security special agents will be assigned to diplomatic missions in 157 countries.*

- *Increased crisis management training programs overseas. This training, coupled with crisis management training provided domestically, helps to ensure that our personnel are fully prepared to respond in future crisis situations.*

This document can be viewed at:

http://www.state.gov/www/global/terrorism/fs_000807_security.html

The increase in the Department's response to the developing threat was also highlighted in the recent statements made to the US Senate. In his Testimony on Counterterrorism before the Senate Appropriations Subcommittee on Commerce, Justice, State and the Judiciary Secretary Colin L. Powell stated:

> *In addition to our prevention efforts, we must also enhance our actual defenses against terrorism as well as our response capabilities.*

> *To protect our installations overseas, our first line of effort is again our ambassadors and their country teams. As we have seen in Nairobi, Dar Es Salaam, Sanaa, Quito, and Manila— to name only a few posts— our Chiefs of Mission, our Ambassadors, are responsible for coordinating the actions of the agencies that work within our embassies to defend against and, when defense fails, to respond to terrorist acts.*

> *With the exception of those people directly under the authority of a regional military CINC, Commander in Chief, our Chiefs of Mission are responsible for all official Americans working on behalf of the American people, whether they are Legal or Defense Attaches, Intelligence Officers, or Foreign Service Officers or Civil Service Officers.*

> *The State Department also leads the Foreign Emergency Support Team, FEST team, which is deployed to serve as an ambassador's consultative and support unit in response to a terrorist attack or sometimes in anticipation of a potential threat. In the past year, this team has been deployed to such far reaches as Manila, Aden, and Quito.*

> *With respect to an actual terrorist incident, this interagency team, led by experienced State Department professionals, plays a crucial role in our response. It helps us ensure that those first days, weeks, and often months after the incident are focused on accomplishing the daunting tasks of securing American lives and assets, taking good care of the people involved, working intimately with the host government to ensure that justice is served, and keeping Washington informed on critical developments.*

> *The State Department also provides excellent physical security for our missions around the world, and we are trying to do an even better job, as I have testified before this committee previously. Our Diplomatic Security corps is watching threats around the clock to ensure that American officials based or traveling abroad are secure. And as you may recall from my budget testimony, we are going to hire more of these professionals with the money that is now in the President's budget request for 2002.*

> *Also from my budget testimony, you know the pace at which we are approaching embassy construction and refurbishment and that this is an additional element of our defense against terrorism.*

So America's international defense and response capabilities are clearly defined, coordinated, and functioning well. We are working closely with our government interagency partners here and abroad. We are constantly reviewing and exercising our response capabilities to ensure they continue to address changing needs.

The leaders of our Foreign Emergency Support Teams head interagency exercises at least twice a year to ensure that our teams are ready for different and changing types of emergency response needs, ranging from airplane hijackings to nuclear blackmail. The composition of the team depends on the incident and includes specialists such as FBI hostage negotiators and forensic experts, or WMD consequence management planners.

State Department officials, both in Washington and abroad, regularly train for emergency response in an interagency environment. We strive to maintain a high level of readiness in our Washington-based taskforces and international emergency action response capabilities.

Our Diplomatic Security people constantly review their extensive programs with other law enforcement agencies and activities to ensure that they develop and maintain the best possible capability to protect our official people and facilities overseas and to ensure that we are adequately protecting Americans abroad.

The full text can be viewed at

http://www.state.gov/s/ct/rls/2001/index.cfm?docid=2780

US Citizens

The responsibility for providing consular protection and services to US citizens abroad resides with the Bureau of Consular Affairs at the Department of State. In April of this year the Director of the Bureau offered the following testimony to the House of Representatives. The full text is available at:

www.house.gov/reform/ns/107th_testimony/andruch_april_3.htm

The portion relevant to the issue of protecting against, or aiding US citizens in a time of, crisis included the following text:

The Bureau of Consular Affairs (CA) is charged with exercising the Secretary of State's responsibility to provide consular protection and services to United States citizens abroad. There is no higher priority of the Department of State than the protection and welfare of Americans overseas.

The Directorate for Overseas Citizens Services (OCS) provides a full range of emergency and non-emergency consular services to Americans residing and traveling abroad. We exercise this responsibility through a staff in Washington and our consular colleagues in our Embassies and Consulates throughout the world. Consular Duty Personnel are available 24 hours a day, 7 days a week in Washington and overseas. OCS provides vital assistance to U.S. citizens abroad on a daily basis and during periods of crisis.

In times of crisis, when Americans are affected by events such as natural disasters, civil unrest, political instability or transportation disasters, OCS coordinates the Consular response in Washington and at our posts abroad. We immediately alert Americans to the existing danger. We oversee the operations of our consular personnel in the affected country and establish and maintain the consular segment of the Washington-based task force. In addition, we provide a vital point of contact for Americans in the U.S. concerned about relatives overseas. We also serve as a focal point for our involved missions to seek guidance and instruction on consular assistance and we collect information on the status of Americans overseas and share it with concerned family members and friends.

Another important aspect of our consular crisis work is assuring that there is adequate consular staffing and resources to manage the problem. We supplement consular staff overseas with temporary help from the U.S. or neighboring posts, maintain crisis teams ready to provide the first response to an emergency, and liaise with other offices in the Department and in the U.S. Government to bring all appropriate resources to bear and to ensure a concerted, coordinated response.

Since the bombings of our Embassies in Nairobi and Dar es Salaam in 1998, we have found it useful to issue Worldwide Caution Public Announcements, to alert Americans generally to the fact that terrorists have threatened action against Americans and American interests abroad. The latest such Announcement was issued on January 1, 2001, and remains in effect.

Other information, particularly that which may pertain to terrorist threats, is obtained from a variety of sources— from the U.S. intelligence community, those of our allies, friendly sources, open threats, etc. No matter what the source all information is taken seriously and put through a comprehensive evaluation process. Before the information is shared with the public, it must meet the three criteria I have just mentioned. It must be specific and credible and non-counterable. This threshold precludes us from publishing unsubstantiated information and suffering the consequences of "crying wolf."

It is therefore clear that the bombings in Kenya and Tanzania had a significant impact on how the Department of State viewed its responsibilities, it did not however prevent the US military and in particular the US Navy from becoming the next target— the attack on the USS Cole in Yemen once again proved that inadequate consideration of risk and absence of detailed planning creates opportunities that terrorists will exploit. In an incident that is strikingly similar to the vehicular attacks on the Embassies, a suicide-terrorist attack crippled a US military asset and killed service personnel.

US Military Assets

In April 2001 the US Navy issued the following statement concerning the USS Cole incident.

The Judge Advocate General Manual (JAGMAN) investigation of the terrorist bombing of USS Cole (DDG 67) during its refueling in Aden, Yemen, Oct. 12, 2000 provides a comprehensive account of the actions taken onboard Cole before, during, and after the terrorist attack that killed 17 Sailors and wounded more than twice that number. JAGMAN investigations provide the Navy an effective means to gather the facts about what happened, determine "lessons learned" to help prevent future such incidents, and assess accountability of those involved as appropriate.

Chief of Naval Operations, Adm. Vern Clark completed the JAGMAN investigation, and agreed with the findings of the Commander in Chief, U.S. Atlantic Fleet, Adm. Robert Natter, that the commanding officer acted reasonably in adjusting his force protection posture based on his assessment of the situation that presented itself when Cole arrived in Aden to refuel.

"I found Adm. Natter's analysis to be both well-reasoned and convincing," Adm. Clark said, "and therefore agreed with his determination that the facts do not warrant any punitive action against the Commanding Officer or other members of Cole's crew."

In assessing the accountability of the commanding officer, the Navy essentially needed to answer two questions: Were the decisions made and the actions taken by the commanding officer reasonable and within the range of performance we expect of our commanders; and would any of the force protection measures **not** *implemented by USS Cole have deterred or defeated this determined attack if they* **had** *been implemented.*

The conclusion of Adm. Natter— agreed to and supported by both the CNO and Secretary of the Navy Richard Danzig— is that the commanding officer's decisions were reasonable and appropriate under the circumstances, and that even perfect implementation of all Force Protection measures specified under Threat Condition Bravo would not have prevented or deterred this attack.

The JAGMAN also pointed to a number of significant "lessons learned" from the incident:

- *The Navy needs to do a better job of both training and equipping its ships to operate with reasonable risk in a high-threat environment.*

- *Collective responsibility exists for oversight in pre-deployment training, threat awareness and in-theater support for entering new ports.*

- *The Navy must — and is — taking force protection to a new level. The Secretary of the Navy's Task Force on Antiterrorism and Force Protection is already spearheading efforts to create a fundamentally improved force protection mindset throughout the Navy, and to challenge every assumption we make about how we conduct naval operations around the globe.*

- *Well-built ships with well-trained crews remain the key to survival, whether the battle is with other military forces or criminal terrorists.*

The Navy leadership also noted that the investigation underscored shortcomings throughout the network of commands, departments and agencies that provide support to U.S. Navy ships operating in foreign waters around the globe.

"The investigation clearly shows that the commanding officer of Cole did not have the specific intelligence, focused training, appropriate equipment or on-scene security support to effectively prevent or deter such a determined, preplanned assault on his ship," Adm. Clark said. "In short, the system— all of us— did not equip this skipper for success in the environment he encountered in Aden harbor that fateful day."

Secretary Danzig underscored the importance of a thorough assessment of accountability in his review of the JAGMAN investigation. "We must account for why 17 people under our charge died, and why many other people, material and interests within our responsibility have been injured," Mr. Danzig said. "In the process we cannot avoid our own responsibility for what the terrorists achieved. We owe it to those who suffer to provide the comfort of explanation, to the best of our abilities."

Current status?

The Current Status of a US-Instigated Response

So what capabilities exist to deal with an emergency overseas?

One of the seminar panelists, Dr. Susan Briggs, described her experiences with the US-based National Disaster Medical System (NDMS). The NDMS is part of the system being developed by the Department of Health and Human Services. It is coordinated through DHHS Office of Emergency Preparedness (OEP).

OEP is an office within the U.S. Department of Health and Human Services and has the Departmental responsibility for managing and coordinating Federal health, medical, and health related social services and recovery to major emergencies and Federally declared disasters including:

- Natural Disasters

- Technological Disasters

- Major Transportation Accidents

- Terrorism

Working in partnership with the Federal Emergency Management Agency (FEMA) and the Federal interagency community, OEP serves as the lead Federal agency for health and medical services within the Federal Response Plan. OEP also directs and manages the National Disaster Medical System (NDMS) a cooperative asset-sharing partnership between HHS, the Department of Defense (DoD), the Department of Veterans Affairs (VA), FEMA, state and local governments, private businesses and civilian volunteers.

OEP is also responsible for Federal health and medical response to terrorist acts involving Weapons of Mass Destruction (WMD).

Their web site is located at: www.ndms.dhhs.gov/index.html

The NDMS is a cooperative asset-sharing program among Federal government agencies, state and local governments, and the private businesses and civilian volunteers to ensure resources are available to provide medical services following a disaster that overwhelms the local health care resources.

The National Disaster Medical System (NDMS) is a Federally coordinated system that augments the Nation's emergency medical response capability. The overall purpose of the NDMS is to establish a single, integrated national medical response capability for assisting state and local authorities in dealing with the medical and health effects of major peacetime disasters and providing support to the military and Veterans Health Administration medical systems in caring for casualties evacuated back to the U.S. from overseas armed conflicts.

The NDMS web site is located at:

www.ndms.dhhs.gov/NDMS/ndms.html

The role of FEMA has been increased with the recent announcement by the President that they will take the lead role in providing for a response in the event of a bioterrorist attack on the U.S. mainland. FEMA is an independent agency of the federal government, reporting to the President. Since its founding in 1979, FEMA's mission has been clear:

> *to reduce loss of life and property and protect our nation's critical infrastructure from all types of hazards through a comprehensive, risk-based, emergency management program of mitigation, preparedness, response and recovery.*

In February 2001, FEMA announced that they, the FBI and five other federal agencies have developed and published a plan for responding to a terrorist threat or incident in the United States. The *U.S. Government Interagency Domestic Terrorism Concept of Operations Plan* outlines how the federal government would respond to a terrorist threat or incident, including one involving weapons of mass destruction. The Departments of Justice, Defense, Energy, Health and Human Services, and the Environmental Protection Agency played key roles in the plan's development, which implements a Presidential directive issued in 1995. The new plan establishes guidelines for assessing and monitoring a threat, notifying the appropriate agencies and deploying resources to coordinate a crisis and consequence management response.

In a terrorist event in the United States, the FBI is the lead agency for *crisis management* while FEMA is the lead agency for *consequence management.* Crisis management primarily refers to law enforcement functions to prevent, preempt, and terminate terrorism and apprehend and prosecute the perpetrators, while consequence management involves the emergency management functions to save lives, protect property, restore government services, and provide emergency relief.

In May 2001 FEMA announced the availability of new terrorism preparedness planning guidance for state and local governments. The terrorism planning guidance provides state and local emergency planners:

- Information and a framework for developing supplemental emergency operations plans to address the consequences of terrorist acts involving weapons of mass destruction; and

- A consistent planning approach to help foster efficient integration of state, local, and federal terrorism consequences management activities.

The new guidance, Attachment G - Terrorism, is a supplement to Chapter 6 of FEMA's State and Local Guide 101, *Guide for All-Hazard Emergency Operations Planning*. The document is posted on the FEMA Web site at www.fema.gov/pte/gaheop.htm.

Part III

Selected Documents

Interagency Domestic Terrorism Concept of Operations Plan

United States Government
January 2001

Foreword

Publication of the United States Government Interagency Domestic Terrorism Concept of Operations Plan (CONPLAN) represents a concerted effort by a number of Federal departments and agencies to work together to achieve a common goal.

The CONPLAN was developed through the efforts of six primary departments and agencies with responsibilities as identified in Presidential Decision Directive/NSC-39 (PDD-39). This plan has been developed consistent with relevant PDDs, Federal law, the Attorney General's Critical Incident Response

Plan, the PDD-39 Domestic Guidelines, and the Federal Response Plan and its Terrorism Incident Annex. The FBI has worked with these departments and agencies to provide a forum to participate in planning and exercise activities in order to develop, maintain, and enhance the Federal response capability.

To ensure the policy in PDD-39 and PDD-62 is implemented in a coordinated manner, the CONPLAN is designed to provide overall guidance to Federal, State and local agencies concerning how the Federal government would respond to a potential or actual terrorist threat or incident that occurs in the United States, particularly one involving Weapons of Mass Destruction (WMD). The CONPLAN outlines an organized and unified capability for a timely, coordinated response by Federal agencies to a terrorist threat or act. It establishes conceptual guidance for assessing and monitoring a developing threat, notifying appropriate Federal, State, and local agencies of the nature of the threat, and deploying the requisite advisory and technical resources to assist the Lead Federal Agency (LFA) in facilitating interdepartmental coordination of crisis and consequence management activities.

Actions will continue to refine and identify the mission, capabilities, and resources of other supporting departments and agencies; and the actions each agency or department must perform during each phase of the response, to include crisis management and consequence management actions that are necessary for chemical, biological, nuclear/radiological, and conventional materials or devices.

Inquiries concerning this CONPLAN should be addressed to the appropriate Lead Agency under this plan:

- Federal Bureau of Investigation, Counterterrorism Division, Domestic Terrorism/Counterterrorism Planning Section, for Crisis Management, or

- Federal Emergency Management Agency, Response and Recovery Directorate, Operations and Planning Division, for Consequence Management.

Letter of Agreement

The United States Government Interagency Domestic Terrorism Concept of Operations Plan, hereafter referred to as the CONPLAN, is designed to provide overall guidance to Federal, State and local agencies concerning how the Federal government would respond to a potential or actual terrorist threat or incident that occurs in the United States, particularly one involving WMD. The following departments and agencies agree to support the overall concept of operations of the CONPLAN in order to carry out their assigned responsibilities under PDD-39 and PDD-62. The departments and agencies also agree to implement national and regional planning efforts and exercise activities in order to maintain the overall Federal response capability. Specifically:

- The Attorney General is responsible for ensuring the development and implementation of policies directed at preventing terrorist attacks domestically, and will undertake the criminal prosecution of these acts of terrorism that violate U.S. law. The Department of Justice has charged the Federal Bureau of Investigation with execution of its LFA responsibilities for the management of a Federal response to terrorist incidents. As the lead agency for crisis management, the FBI will implement a Federal crisis management response. As LFA, the FBI will designate a Federal on-scene commander (OSC) to ensure appropriate coordination of the overall United States Government response with Federal, State and local authorities until such time as the Attorney General transfers the LFA role to the Federal Emergency Management Agency (FEMA).

- As the lead agency for consequence management, FEMA will implement the Federal Response Plan (FRP) to manage and coordinate the Federal consequence management response in support of State and local authorities.

- The Department of Defense will provide military assistance to the LFA and/or the CONPLAN primary agencies during all aspects of a terrorist incident upon request by the appropriate authority and approval by the Secretary of Defense.

- The Department of Energy will provide scientific-technical personnel and equipment in support of the LFA during all aspects of a nuclear/radiological WMD terrorist incident.

- The Environmental Protection Agency will provide technical personnel and supporting equipment to the LFA during all aspects of a WMD terrorist incident.

- The Department of Health and Human Services is the primary agency to plan and to prepare for a national response to medical emergencies arising from the terrorist use of WMD. HHS provides technical personnel and supporting equipment to the LFA during all aspects of a terrorist incident.

Signatories to the United States Government Interagency Domestic Terrorism Concept of Operations Plan

I. Introduction and Background

A. Introduction

The ability of the United States Government to prevent, deter, defeat and respond decisively to terrorist attacks against our citizens, whether these attacks occur domestically, in international waters or airspace, or on foreign soil, is one of the most challenging priorities facing our nation today. The United States regards all such terrorism as a potential threat to national security, as well as a violent criminal act, and will apply all appropriate means to combat this danger. In doing so, the United States vigorously pursues efforts to deter and preempt these crimes and to apprehend and prosecute directly, or assist other governments in prosecuting, individuals who perpetrate or plan such terrorist attacks.

In 1995, President Clinton signed Presidential Decision Directive 39 (PDD-39), the United States Policy on Counterterrorism. This Presidential Directive built upon previous directives for combating terrorism and further elaborated a strategy and an interagency coordination mechanism and management structure to be undertaken by the Federal government to combat both domestic and international terrorism in all its forms. This authority includes implementing measures to reduce our vulnerabilities, deterring terrorism through a clear public position, responding rapidly and effectively to threats or actual terrorist acts, and giving the highest priority to developing sufficient capabilities to combat and manage the consequences of terrorist incidents involving weapons of mass destruction (WMD).

To ensure this policy is implemented in a coordinated manner, the Concept of Operations Plan, hereafter referred to as the CONPLAN, is designed to provide overall guidance to Federal, State and local agencies concerning how the Federal government would respond to a potential or actual terrorist threat or incident that occurs in the United States, particularly one involving WMD. The CONPLAN outlines an organized and unified capability for a timely, coordinated response by Federal agencies to a terrorist threat or act. It establishes conceptual guidance for assessing and monitoring a developing threat, notifying appropriate Federal, State, and local agencies of the nature of the threat, and deploying the requisite advisory and technical resources to assist the Lead Federal Agency (LFA) in facilitating interagency/interdepartmental coordination of a crisis and consequence management response. Lastly, it defines the relationships between structures under which the Federal government will marshal crisis and consequence management resources to respond to a threatened or actual terrorist incident.

B.   Purpose

The purpose of this plan is to facilitate an effective Federal, response to all threats or acts of terrorism within the United States that are determined to be of sufficient magnitude to warrant implementation of this plan and the associated policy guidelines established in PDD-39 and PDD-62. To accomplish this, the CONPLAN:

- Establishes a structure for a systematic, coordinated and effective national response to threats or acts of terrorism in the United States;

- Defines procedures for the use of Federal resources to augment and support local and State governments; and

- Encompasses both crisis and consequence management responsibilities, and articulates the coordination relationships between these missions.

C.   Scope

The CONPLAN is a strategic document that:

- Applies to all threats or acts of terrorism within the United States;

- Provides planning guidance and outlines operational concepts for the Federal crisis and consequence management response to a threatened or actual terrorist incident within the United States;

- Serves as the foundation for further development of detailed national, regional, State, and local operations plans and procedures;

- Includes guidelines for notification, coordination and leadership of response activities, supporting operations, and coordination of emergency public information across all levels of government;

- Acknowledges the unique nature of each incident, the capabilities of the local jurisdiction, and the activities necessary to prevent or mitigate a specific threat or incident; and

- Illustrates ways in which Federal, State and local agencies can most effectively unify and synchronize their response actions.

D. Primary Federal Agencies

The response to a terrorist threat or incident within the U.S. will entail a highly coordinated, multi-agency local, State, and Federal response. In support of this mission, the following primary Federal agencies will provide the core Federal response:

- Department of Justice (DOJ) / Federal Bureau of Investigation (FBI)*

- Federal Emergency Management Agency (FEMA) **

- Department of Defense (DOD)

- Department of Energy (DOE)

- Environmental Protection Agency (EPA)

- Department of Health and Human Services (DHHS)

  * Lead Agency for Crisis Management

  ** Lead Agency for Consequence Management

Although not formally designated under the CONPLAN, other Federal departments and agencies may have authorities, resources, capabilities, or expertise required to support response operations. Agencies may be requested to participate in Federal planning and response operations, and may be asked to designate staff to function as liaison officers and provide other support to the LFA.

E. Primary Agency Responsibilities

1. Department of Justice (DOJ)/Federal Bureau of Investigation (FBI)

The Attorney General is responsible for ensuring the development and implementation of policies directed at preventing terrorist attacks domestically, and will undertake the criminal prosecution of these acts of terrorism that violate U.S. law. DOJ has charged the FBI with execution of its LFA responsibilities for the management of a Federal response to terrorist threats or incidents that take place within U.S. territory or those occurring in international waters that do not involve the flag vessel of a foreign country. As the lead agency for crisis management, the FBI will implement a Federal crisis management response. As LFA, the FBI will designate a Federal on-scene commander to ensure appropriate coordination of the overall United States Government response with Federal, State and local authorities until such time as the Attorney General transfers the overall LFA role to FEMA. The FBI, with appropriate approval, will form and coordinate the deployment of a Domestic Emergency Support Team (DEST) with other agencies, when appropriate, and seek appropriate Federal support based on the nature of the situation.

2. Federal Emergency Management Agency (FEMA)

As the lead agency for consequence management, FEMA will manage and coordinate any Federal consequence management response in support of State and local governments in accordance with its statutory authorities. Additionally, FEMA will designate appropriate liaison and advisory personnel for the FBI's Strategic Information and Operations Center (SIOC) and deployment with the DEST, the Joint Operations Center (JOC), and the Joint Information Center (JIC).

3. Department of Defense (DOD)

DOD serves as a support agency to the FBI for crisis management functions, including technical operations, and a support agency to FEMA for consequence management. In accordance with DOD Directives 3025.15 and 2000.12 and the Chairman Joint Chiefs of Staff CONPLAN 0300-97, and upon approval by the Secretary of Defense, DOD will provide assistance to the LFA and/or the CONPLAN primary agencies, as appropriate, during all aspects of a terrorist incident, including both crisis and consequence management. DOD assistance includes threat assessment; DEST participation and transportation; technical advice; operational support; tactical support; support for civil disturbances; custody, transportation and disposal of a WMD device; and other capabilities including mitigation of the consequences of a release.

DOD has many unique capabilities for dealing with a WMD and combating terrorism, such as the US Army Medical Research Institute for Infectious Diseases, Technical Escort Unit, and US Marine Corps Chemical Biological Incident Response Force. These and other DOD assets may be used in responding to a terrorist incident if requested by the LFA and approved by the Secretary of Defense.

4.   Department of Energy (DOE)

DOE serves as a support agency to the FBI for technical operations and a support agency to FEMA for consequence management. DOE provides scientific-technical personnel and equipment in support of the LFA during all aspects of a nuclear/radiological WMD terrorist incident. DOE assistance can support both crisis and consequence management activities with capabilities such as threat assessment, DEST deployment, LFA advisory requirements, technical advice, forecasted modeling predictions, and operational support to include direct support of tactical operations. Deployable DOE scientific technical assistance and support includes capabilities such as search operations; access operations; diagnostic and device assessment; radiological assessment and monitoring; identification of material; development of Federal protective action recommendations; provision of information on the radiological response; render safe operations; hazards assessment; containment, relocation and storage of special nuclear material evidence; post-incident clean-up; and on-site management and radiological assessment to the public, the White House, and members of Congress and foreign governments. All DOE support to a Federal response will be coordinated through a Senior Energy Official.

5.   Environmental Protection Agency (EPA)

EPA serves as a support agency to the FBI for technical operations and a support agency to FEMA for consequence management. EPA provides technical personnel and supporting equipment to the LFA during all aspects of a WMD terrorist incident. EPA assistance may include threat assessment, DEST and regional emergency response team deployment, LFA advisory requirements, technical advice and operational support for chemical, biological, and radiological releases. EPA assistance and advice includes threat assessment, consultation, agent identification, hazard detection and reduction, environmental monitoring; sample and forensic evidence collection/analysis; identification of contaminants; feasibility assessment and clean-up; and on-site safety, protection, prevention, decontamination, and restoration activities. EPA and the United States Coast Guard (USCG) share responsibilities for response to oil discharges into navigable waters and releases of hazardous substances, pollutants, and contaminants into the environment under the National Oil and Hazardous Substances Pollution Contingency Plan (NCP). EPA provides the predesignated Federal On-Scene Coordinator for inland areas and the USCG for coastal areas to coordinate containment, removal, and disposal efforts and resources during an oil, hazardous substance, or WMD incident.

6.   Department of Health and Human Services (HHS)

HHS serves as a support agency to the FBI for technical operations and a support agency to FEMA for consequence management. HHS provides technical personnel and supporting equipment to the LFA during all aspects of a terrorist incident. HHS can also provide regulatory follow-up when an incident involves a product regulated by the Food and Drug Administration. HHS assistance supports threat assessment, DEST deployment, epidemiological investigation, LFA advisory requirements, and technical advice. Technical assistance to the FBI may include identification of agents, sample collection and analysis, on-site safety and protection activities, and medical management planning. Operational support to FEMA may include mass immunization, mass prophylaxis, mass fatality management, pharmaceutical support operations (National Pharmaceutical Stockpile), contingency medical records, patient tracking, and patient evacuation and definitive medical care provided through the National Disaster Medical System.

II. Policies

A. Authorities

The following authorities are the basis for the development of the CONPLAN:

- Presidential Decision Directive 39, including the Domestic Guidelines Presidential Decision Directive 62

- Robert T. Stafford Disaster Relief and Emergency Assistance Act

B. Other Plans and Directives

Federal Response Plan, including the Terrorism Incident Annex, Federal Radiological Emergency Response Plan, National Oil and Hazardous Substances Pollution Contingency Plan, HHS Health and Medical Services Support Plan for the Federal Response to Assets of Chemical/Biological Terrorism, Chairman of the Joint Chiefs of Staff CONPLAN 0300/0400 DODD 3025.15 Military Assistance to Civil Authorities, other Department of Defense Directives.

C. Federal Agency Authorities

The CONPLAN does not supersede existing plans or authorities that were developed for response to incidents under department and agency statutory authorities. Rather, it is intended to be a coordinating plan between crisis and consequence management to provide an effective Federal response to terrorism. The CONPLAN is a Federal signatory plan among the six principal departments and agencies named in PDD-39. It may be updated and amended, as necessary, by consensus among these agencies.

D. Federal Response to a Terrorism Incident

The Federal response to a terrorist threat or incident provides a tailored, time-phased deployment of specialized Federal assets. The response is executed under two broad responsibilities:

1.   Crisis Management

Crisis management is predominantly a law enforcement function and includes measures to identify, acquire, and plan the use of resources needed to anticipate, prevent, and/or resolve a threat or act of terrorism. In a terrorist incident, a crisis management response may include traditional law enforcement missions, such as intelligence, surveillance, tactical operations, negotiations, forensics, and investigations, as well as technical support missions, such as agent identification, search, render safe procedures, transfer and disposal, and limited decontamination. In addition to the traditional law enforcement missions, crisis management also includes assurance of public health and safety.

The laws of the United States assign primary authority to the Federal government to prevent and respond to acts of terrorism or potential acts of terrorism. Based on the situation, a Federal crisis management response may be supported by technical operations, and by consequence management activities, which should operate concurrently.

2.   Consequence Management

Consequence management is predominantly an emergency management function and includes measures to protect public health and safety, restore essential government services, and provide emergency relief to governments, businesses, and individuals affected by the consequences of terrorism. In an actual or potential terrorist incident, a consequence management response will be managed by FEMA using structures and resources of the Federal Response Plan (FRP). These efforts will include support missions as described in other Federal operations plans, such as predictive modeling, protective action recommendations, and mass decontamination.

The laws of the United States assign primary authority to the State and local governments to respond to the consequences of terrorism; the Federal government provides assistance, as required.

E.   *Lead Federal Agency Designation*

As mandated by the authorities referenced above, the operational response to a terrorist threat will employ a coordinated, interagency process organized through a LFA concept. PDD-39 reaffirms and elaborates on the U.S. Government's policy on counterterrorism and expands the roles, responsibilities and management structure for combating terrorism. LFA responsibility is assigned to the Department of Justice, and is delegated to the FBI, for threats or acts of terrorism that take place in the United States or in international waters that do not involve the flag vessel of a foreign country. Within this role, the FBI Federal on-scene commander (OSC) will function as the on-scene manager for the U.S. Government. All Federal agencies and departments, as needed, will support the Federal OSC. Threats or acts of terrorism that take place outside of the United States or its trust territories, or in international waters and involve the flag vessel of a foreign country are outside the scope of the CONPLAN.

In addition, these authorities reaffirm that FEMA is the lead agency for consequence management within U.S. territory. FEMA retains authority and responsibility to act as the lead agency for consequence management throughout the Federal response. FEMA will use the FRP structure to coordinate all Federal assistance to State and local governments for consequence management. To ensure that there is one overall LFA, PDD-39 directs FEMA to support the Department of Justice (as delegated to the FBI) until the Attorney General transfers the LFA role to FEMA. At such time, the responsibility to function as the on-scene manager for the U.S. Government transfers from the FBI Federal OSC to the Federal Coordinating Officer (FCO).

F.   Requests For Federal Assistance

Requests for Federal assistance by State and local governments, as well as those from owners and operators of critical infrastructure facilities, are coordinated with the lead agency (crisis or consequence) responsible under U.S. law for that function. In response to a terrorist threat or incident, multiple or competing requests will be managed based on priorities and objectives established by the JOC Command Group.

State and local governments will submit requests for Federal crisis management assistance through the FBI. State and local governments will submit requests for Federal consequence management assistance through standard channels under the Federal Response Plan. FEMA liaisons assigned to the DEST or JOC coordinate requests with the LFA to ensure consequence management plans and actions are consistent with overall priorities. All other requests for consequence management assistance submitted outside normal channels to the DEST or JOC will be forwarded to the Regional Operations Center (ROC) Director or the Federal Coordinating Officer (FCO) for action.

G.   Funding

As mandated by PDD-39, Federal agencies directed to participate in counterterrorist operations or the resolution of terrorist incidents bear the costs of their own participation, unless otherwise directed by the President. This responsibility is subject to specific statutory authorization to provide support without reimbursement. In the absence of such specific authority, the Economy Act applies, and reimbursement cannot be waived.

H.   Deployment/Employment Priorities

The multi-agency JOC Command Group, managed by the Federal OSC, ensures that conflicts are resolved, overall incident objectives are established, and strategies are selected for the use of critical resources. These strategies will be based on the following priorities:

- Preserving life or minimizing risk to health. This constitutes the first priority of operations.

- Preventing a threatened act from being carried out or an existing terrorist act from being expanded or aggravated.

- Locating, accessing, rendering safe, controlling, containing, recovering, and disposing of a WMD that has not yet functioned.

- Rescuing, decontaminating, transporting and treating victims. Preventing secondary casualties as a result of contamination or collateral threats.

- Releasing emergency public information that ensures adequate and accurate communications with the public from all involved response agencies.

- Restoring essential services and mitigating suffering.

- Apprehending and successfully prosecuting perpetrators.

- Conducting site restoration.

I.   Planning Assumptions and Considerations

1.   The CONPLAN assumes that no single private or government agency at the local, State, or Federal level possesses the authority and the expertise to act unilaterally on the difficult issues that may arise in response to threats or acts of terrorism, particularly if nuclear, radiological, biological, or chemical materials are involved.

2.   The CONPLAN is based on the premise that a terrorist incident may occur at any time of day with little or no warning, may involve single or multiple geographic areas, and result in mass casualties.

3.   The CONPLAN also assumes an act of terrorism, particularly an act directed against a large population center within the United States involving nuclear, radiological, biological, or chemical materials, will have major consequences that can overwhelm the capabilities of many local and State governments to respond and may seriously challenge existing Federal response capabilities, as well.

4.   Federal participating agencies may need to respond on short notice to provide effective and timely assistance to State and local governments.

5.   Federal departments and agencies would be expected to provide an initial response when warranted under their own authorities and funding. Decisions to mobilize Federal assets will be coordinated with the FBI and FEMA.

6.   In the case of a biological WMD attack, the effect may be temporally and geographically dispersed, with no determined or defined "incident site." Response operations may be conducted over a multi-jurisdictional, multi-State region.

7.   A biological WMD attack employing a contagious agent may require quarantine by State and local health officials to contain the disease outbreak.

8.   Local, State, and Federal responders will define working perimeters that overlap. Perimeters may be used by responders to control access to an affected area, to assign operational sectors among responding organizations, and to assess potential effects on the population and the environment. Control of these perimeters and response actions may be managed by different authorities, which will impede the effectiveness of the overall response if adequate coordination is not established.

9.   If appropriate personal protective equipment and capabilities are not available and the area is contaminated with WMD materials, it is possible that response actions into a contaminated area may be delayed until the material has dissipated to a level that is safe for emergency response personnel to operate.

J.   Training and Exercises

Federal agencies, in conjunction with State and local governments, will periodically exercise their roles and responsibilities designated under the CONPLAN. Federal agencies should coordinate their exercises with the Exercise Subgroup of the Interagency Working Group on Counterterrorism and other response agencies to avoid duplication, and, more importantly, to provide a forum to exercise coordination mechanisms among responding agencies.

Federal agencies will assist State and local governments design and improve their response capabilities to a terrorist threat or incident. Each agency should coordinate its training programs with other response agencies to avoid duplication and to make its training available to other agencies.

III. Situation

A. *Introduction*

The complexity, scope, and potential consequences of a terrorist threat or incident require that there be a rapid and decisive capability to resolve the situation. The resolution to an act of terrorism demands an extraordinary level of coordination of crisis and consequence management functions and technical expertise across all levels of government. No single Federal, State, or local governmental agency has the capability or requisite authority to respond independently and mitigate the consequences of such a threat to national security. The incident may affect a single location or multiple locations, each of which may be a disaster scene, a hazardous scene and/or a crime scene simultaneously.

B. *Differences Between WMD Incidents and Other Incidents*

As in all incidents, WMD incidents may involve mass casualties and damage to buildings or other types of property. However, there are several factors surrounding WMD incidents that are unlike any other type of incidents that must be taken into consideration when planning a response. First responders' ability to identify aspects of the incident (e.g., signs and symptoms exhibited by victims) and report them accurately will be key to maximizing the use of critical local resources and for triggering a Federal response.

1. The situation may not be recognizable until there are multiple casualties. Most chemical and biological agents are not detectable by methods used for explosives and firearms. Most agents can be carried in containers that look like ordinary items.

2. There may be multiple events (e.g., one event in an attempt to influence another event's outcome).

3. Responders are placed at a higher risk of becoming casualties. Because agents are not readily identifiable, responders may become contaminated before recognizing the agent involved. First responders may, in addition, be targets for secondary releases or explosions.

4. The location of the incident will be treated as a crime scene. As such, preservation and collection of evidence is critical. Therefore, it is important to ensure that actions on-scene are coordinated between response organizations to minimize any conflicts between law enforcement authorities, who view the incident as a crime scene, and other responders, who view it as a hazardous materials or disaster scene.

5. Contamination of critical facilities and large geographic areas may result. Victims may carry an agent unknowingly to public transportation facilities, businesses, residences, doctors' offices, walk-in medical clinics, or emergency rooms because they don't realize that they are contaminated. First responders may carry the agent to fire or precinct houses, hospitals, or to the locations of subsequent calls.

6. The scope of the incident may expand geometrically and may affect mutual aid jurisdictions. Airborne agents flow with the air current and may disseminate via ventilation systems, carrying the agents far from the initial source.

7. There will be a stronger reaction from the public than with other types of incidents. The thought of exposure to a chemical or biological agent or radiation evokes terror in most people. The fear of the unknown also makes the public's response more severe.

8. Time is working against responding elements. The incident can expand geometrically and very quickly. In addition, the effects of some chemicals and biological agents worsen over time.

9. Support facilities, such as utility stations and 911 centers along with critical infrastructures, are at risk as targets.

10. Specialized State and local response capabilities may be overwhelmed.

C. Threat Levels

The CONPLAN establishes a range of threat levels determined by the FBI that serve to frame the nature and scope of the Federal response. Each threat level provides for an escalating range of actions that will be implemented concurrently for crisis and consequence management. The Federal government will take specific actions which are synchronized to each threat level, ensuring that all Federal agencies are operating with jointly and consistently executed plans. The Federal government will notify and coordinate with State and local governments, as necessary. The threat levels are described below:

1. Level #4 - Minimal Threat:

Received threats do not warrant actions beyond normal liaison notifications or placing assets or resources on a heightened alert (agencies are operating under normal day-to-day conditions).

2.   Level #3 - Potential Threat:

Intelligence or an articulated threat indicates a potential for a terrorist incident. However, this threat has not yet been assessed as credible.

3.   Level #2 - Credible Threat:

A threat assessment indicates that the potential threat is credible, and confirms the involvement of WMD in the developing terrorist incident. Intelligence will vary with each threat, and will impact the level of the Federal response. At this threat level, the situation requires the tailoring of response actions to use Federal resources needed to anticipate, prevent, and/or resolve the crisis. The Federal crisis management response will focus on law enforcement actions taken in the interest of public safety and welfare, and is predominantly concerned with preventing and resolving the threat. The Federal consequence management response will focus on contingency planning and pre-positioning of tailored resources, as required. The threat increases in significance when the presence of an explosive device or WMD capable of causing a significant destructive event, prior to actual injury or loss, is confirmed or when intelligence and circumstances indicate a high probability that a device exists. In this case, the threat has developed into a WMD terrorist situation requiring an immediate process to identify, acquire, and plan the use of Federal resources to augment State and local authorities in lessening or averting the potential consequence of a terrorist use or employment of WMD.

4.   Level #1 - WMD Incident:

A WMD terrorism incident has occurred which requires an immediate process to identify, acquire, and plan the use of Federal resources to augment State and local authorities in response to limited or major consequences of a terrorist use or employment of WMD. This incident has resulted in mass casualties. The Federal response is primarily directed toward public safety and welfare and the preservation of human life.

D.   *Lead Federal Agency Responsibilities*

The LFA, in coordination with the appropriate Federal, State and local agencies, is responsible for formulating the Federal strategy and a coordinated Federal response. To accomplish that goal, the LFA must establish multi-agency coordination structures, as appropriate, at the incident scene, area, and national level. These structures are needed to perform oversight responsibilities in operations involving multiple agencies with direct statutory authority to respond to aspects of a single major incident or multiple incidents. Oversight responsibilities include:

•   Coordination. Coordinate the determination of operational objectives, strategies, and priorities for the use of critical resources that have been allocated to the situation, and communicate multi-agency decisions back to individual agencies and incidents.

- Situation Assessment. Evaluate emerging threats, prioritize incidents, and project future needs.

- Public Information. As the spokesperson for the Federal response, the LFA is responsible for coordinating information dissemination to the White House, Congress, and other Federal, State and local government officials. In fulfilling this responsibility, the LFA ensures that the release of public information is coordinated between crisis and consequence management response entities. The Joint Information Center (JIC) is established by the LFA, under the operational control of the LFA's Public Information Officer, as a focal point for the coordination and provision of information to the public and media concerning the Federal response to the emergency. The JIC may be established in the same location as the FBI Joint Operations Center (JOC) or may be located at an on-scene location in coordination with State and local agencies. The following elements should be represented at the JIC: (1) FBI Public Information Officer and staff, (2) FEMA Public Information Officer and staff, (3) other Federal agency Public Information Officers, as needed, and (4) State and local Public Information Officers.

IV. Concept of Operations

A. Mission

The overall Lead Federal Agency, in conjunction with the lead agencies for crisis and consequence management response, and State and local authorities where appropriate, will notify, activate, deploy and employ Federal resources in response to a threat or act of terrorism. Operations will be conducted in accordance with statutory authorities and applicable plans and procedures, as modified by the policy guidelines established in PDD-39 and PDD-62. The overall LFA will continue operations until the crisis is resolved. Operations under the CONPLAN will then stand down, while operations under other Federal plans may continue to assist State and local governments with recovery.

B. Command and Control

Command and control of a terrorist threat or incident is a critical function that demands a unified framework for the preparation and execution of plans and orders. Emergency response organizations at all levels of government may manage command and control activities somewhat differently depending on the organization's history, the complexity of the crisis, and their capabilities and resources. Management of Federal, State and local response actions must, therefore, reflect an inherent flexibility in order to effectively address the entire spectrum of capabilities and resources across the United States. The resulting challenge is to integrate the different types of management systems and approaches utilized by all levels of government into a comprehensive and unified response to meet the unique needs and requirements of each incident.

I. Consequence Management

State and local consequence management organizations are generally structured to respond to an incident scene using a modular, functionally-oriented ICS that can be tailored to the kind, size and management needs of the incident. ICS is employed to organize and unify multiple disciplines with multi-jurisdictional responsibilities on-scene under one functional organization. State and local emergency operations plans generally establish direction and control procedures for their agencies' response to disaster situations. The organization's staff is built from a "top-down" approach with responsibility and authority placed initially with an Incident Commander who determines which local resources will be deployed. In many States, State law or local jurisdiction ordinances will identify by organizational position the person(s) that will be responsible for serving as the incident commander. In most cases, the incident commander will come from the State or local organization that has primary responsibility for managing the emergency situation.

When the magnitude of a crisis exceeds the capabilities and resources of the local incident commander or multiple jurisdictions become involved in order to resolve the crisis situation, the ICS command function can readily evolve into a Unified Command (see Figure 1). Under Unified Command, a multi-agency command post is established incorporating officials from agencies with jurisdictional responsibility at the incident scene. Multiple agency resources and personnel will then be integrated into the ICS as the single overall response management structure at the incident scene.

Multi-agency coordination to provide resources to support on-scene operations in complex or multiple incidents is the responsibility of emergency management. In the emergency management system, requests for resources are filled at the lowest possible level of government. Requests that exceed available capabilities are progressively forwarded until filled, from a local Emergency Operations Center (EOC), to a State EOC, to Federal operations centers at the regional or national level.

State assistance may be provided to local governments in responding to a terrorist threat or recovering from the consequences of a terrorist incident as in any natural or man-made disaster. The governor, by State law, is the chief executive officer of the State or commonwealth and has full authority to discharge the duties of his office and exercise all powers associated with the operational control of the State's emergency services during a declared emergency. State agencies are responsible for ensuring that essential services and resources are available to the local authorities and Incident Commander when requested. When State assistance is provided, the local government retains overall responsibility for command and control of the emergency operations, except in cases where State or Federal statutes transfer authority to a specific State or Federal agency. State and local governments have primary responsibility for consequence management. FEMA, using the FRP, directs and coordinates all Federal response efforts to manage the consequences in domestic incidents, for which the President has declared, or expressed an intent to declare, an emergency.

2. Crisis Management

As the lead agency for crisis management, the FBI manages a crisis situation from an FBI command post or JOC, bringing the necessary assets to respond and resolve the threat or incident. These activities primarily coordinate the law enforcement actions responding to the cause of the incident with State and local agencies.

During a crisis situation, the FBI Special Agent In Charge (SAC) of the local Field Division will establish a command post to manage the threat based upon a graduated and flexible response. This command post structure generally consists of three functional groups, Command, Operations, and Support, and is designed to accommodate participation of other agencies, as appropriate (see Figure 2). When the threat or incident exceeds the capabilities and resources of the local FBI Field Division, the SAC can request additional resources from the FBI's Critical Incident Response Group, located at Quantico, VA, to augment existing crisis management capabilities. In a terrorist threat or incident that may involve a WMD, the traditional FBI command post is expanded into a JOC incorporating a fourth functional entity, the Consequence Management Group.

Requests for DOD assistance for crisis management during the incident come from the Attorney General to the Secretary of Defense through the DOD Executive Secretary. Once the Secretary has approved the request, the order will be transmitted either directly to the unit involved or through the Chairman of the Joint Chiefs of Staff.

C. Unification of Federal, State and Local Response

I. Introduction

Throughout the management of the terrorist incident, crisis and consequence management components will operate concurrently (see Figure 3). The concept of operations for a Federal response to a terrorist threat or incident provides for the designation of an LFA to ensure multi-agency coordination and a tailored, time-phased deployment of specialized Federal assets. It is critical that all participating Federal, State, and local agencies interact in a seamless manner.

2.   National Level Coordination

The complexity and potential catastrophic consequences of a terrorist event will require application of a multi-agency coordination system at the Federal agency headquarters level. Many critical on-scene decisions may need to be made in consultation with higher authorities. In addition, the transfer of information between the headquarters and field levels is critical to the successful resolution of the crisis incident.

Upon determination of a credible threat, FBI Headquarters (FBIHQ) will activate its Strategic Information and Operations Center (SIOC) to coordinate and manage the national level support to a terrorism incident. At this level, the SIOC will generally mirror the JOC structure operating in the field. The SIOC is staffed by liaison officers from other Federal agencies that are required to provide direct support to the FBI, in accordance with PDD-39. The SIOC performs the critical functions of coordinating the Federal response and facilitating Federal agency headquarters connectivity. Affected Federal agencies will operate headquarters-level emergency operations centers, as necessary.

Upon notification by the FBI of a credible terrorist threat, FEMA may activate its Catastrophic Disaster Response Group. In addition, FEMA will activate the Regional Operations Center and Emergency Support Team, as required.

3.   Field Level Coordination

During a terrorist incident, the organizational structure to implement the Federal response at the field level is the JOC. The JOC is established by the FBI under the operational control of the Federal OSC, and acts as the focal point for the strategic management and direction of on-site activities, identification of State and local requirements and priorities, and coordination of the Federal response. The local FBI field office will activate a Crisis Management Team to establish the JOC, which will be in the affected area, possibly collocated with an existing emergency operations facility. Additionally, the JOC will be augmented by outside agencies, including representatives from the DEST (if deployed), who provide interagency technical expertise as well as inter-agency continuity during the transition from an FBI command post structure to the JOC structure.

Similar to the Area Command concept within the ICS, the JOC is established to ensure inter-incident coordination and to organize multiple agencies and jurisdictions within an overall command and coordination structure. The JOC includes the following functional groups: Command,

Operations, Admin/Logistics, and Consequence Management (see Figure 4). Representation within the JOC includes officials from local, State and Federal agencies with specific roles in crisis and consequence management.

The Command Group of the JOC is responsible for providing recommendations and advice to the Federal OSC regarding the development and implementation of strategic decisions to resolve the crisis situation and for approving the deployment and employment of resources. In this scope, the members of the Command Group play an important role in ensuring the coordination of Federal crisis and consequence management functions. The Command Group is composed of the FBI Federal OSC and senior officials with decision making authority from local, State, and Federal agencies, as appropriate, based upon the circumstances of the threat or incident. Strategies, tactics and priorities are jointly determined within this group. While the FBI retains authority to make Federal crisis management decisions at all times, operational decisions are made cooperatively to the greatest extent possible. The FBI Federal OSC and the senior FEMA official at the JOC will provide, or obtain from higher authority, an immediate resolution of conflicts in priorities for allocation of critical Federal resources between the crisis and consequence management responses.

A FEMA representative coordinates the actions of the JOC Consequence Management Group, and expedites activation of a Federal consequence management response should it become necessary. FBI and FEMA representatives will screen threat/incident intelligence for the Consequence Management Group. The JOC Consequence Management Group monitors the crisis management response in order to advise on decisions that may have implications for consequence management, and to provide continuity should a Federal consequence management response become necessary.

Should the threat of a terrorist incident become imminent, the JOC Consequence Management Group may forward recommendations to the ROC Director to initiate limited pre-deployment of assets under the Stafford Act. Authority to make decisions regarding FRP operations rests with the ROC Director until an FCO is appointed. The senior FEMA official in the JOC ensures appropriate coordination between FRP operations and the JOC Command Group.

4. On-Scene Coordination

Once a WMD incident has occurred (with or without a pre-release crisis period), local government emergency response organizations will respond to the incident scene and appropriate notifications to local, State, and Federal authorities will be made. Control of this incident scene will be established by local response authorities (likely a senior fire or law enforcement official). Command and control of the incident scene is vested with the Incident Commander/Unified Command. Operational control of assets at the sceneisretained by the designated officials representing the agency (local, State, or Federal) providing the assets. These officials manage tactical operations at the scene in coordination with the UC as directed by their agency counterparts at field-level operational centers, if used. As mutual aid partners, State and Federal responders arrive to augment the local responders. The incident command structure that was initially established will likely transition into a Unified Command (UC). This UC structure will facilitate both crisis and consequence management activities. The UC structure used at the scene will expand as support units and agency representatives arrive to support crisis and consequence management operations. On-scene consequence management activities will be supported by the local and State EOC, which will be augmented by the ROC or Disaster Field Office, and the Emergency Support Team, as appropriate.

When Federal resources arrive at the scene, they will operate as a Forward Coordinating Team (FCT). The senior FBI representative will join the Unified Command group while the senior FEMA representative will coordinate activity of Federal consequence management liaisons to the Unified Command. On-scene Federal crisis management resources will be organized into a separate FBI Crisis Management Branch within the Operations Section, and an FBI representative will serve as Deputy to the Operations Section Chief. Federal consequence management resources will assist the appropriate ICS function, as directed (see Figure 5).

Throughout the incident, the actions and activities of the Unified Command at the incident scene and the Command Group of the JOC will be continuously and completely coordinated.

V.   Phasing of the Federal Response

Phasing of the Federal response to a threat or act of terrorism includes Notification; Activation and Deployment; Response Operations; Response Deactivation; and Recovery. Phases may be abbreviated or bypassed when warranted.

A.   Notification

Receipt of a terrorist threat or incident may be through any source or medium, may be articulated, or developed through intelligence sources. It is the responsibility of all local, State, and Federal agencies and departments to notify the FBI when such a threat is received.

Upon receipt of a threat of domestic terrorism, the FBI will conduct a formal threat credibility assessment of the information with assistance from select interagency experts. For a WMD threat, this includes three perspectives:

- Technical feasibility: An assessment of the capacity of the threatening individual or organization to obtain or produce the material at issue;

- Operational practicability: An assessment of the feasibility of delivering or employing the material in the manner threatened;

- Behavioral resolve: A psychological assessment of the likelihood that the subject(s) will carry out the threat, including a review of any written or verbal statement by the subject(s).

The FBI manages a Terrorist Threat Warning System to ensure that vital information regarding terrorism reaches those in the U.S. counterterrorism and law enforcement community responsible for countering terrorist threats. This information is transmitted via secure teletype. Each message transmitted under this system is an alert, an advisory, or an assessment— an alert if the terrorist threat is credible and specific; an advisory if the threat is credible but general in both timing and target; or an assessment to impart facts and/or threat analysis concerning terrorism.

1. The role of the FBI is to:

    a. Verify the accuracy of the notification,

    b. Initiate the threat assessment process,

    c. Notify Domestic Emergency Support Team agencies, and

    d. Notify other Federal, State and local agencies, as appropriate.

2. The role of FEMA is to:

    a. Advise the FBI of consequence management considerations,

    b. Verify that the State and local governments have been notified, and

    c. Notify other Federal agencies under the FRP, as appropriate.

B. Activation and Deployment

Upon determination that the threat is credible, or an act of terrorism has occurred, FBIHQ will initiate appropriate liaison with other Federal agencies to activate their operations centers and provide liaison officers to the SIOC. In addition, FBIHQ will initiate communications with the SAC of the responsible Field Office apprising him/her of possible courses of action and discussing deployment of the DEST. The FBI SAC will establish initial operational priorities based upon the specific circumstances of the threat or incident. This information will then be forwarded to FBIHQ to coordinate identification and deployment of appropriate resources.

Based upon a credible threat assessment and a request by the SAC, the FBI Director, in consultation with the Attorney General, may request authorization through National Security Council groups to deploy the DEST to assist the SAC in mitigating the crisis situation. The DEST is a rapidly deployable, inter-agency team responsible for providing the FBI expert advice and support concerning the U.S. Government's capabilities in resolving the terrorist threat or incident. This includes crisis and consequence management assistance, technical or scientific advice and contingency planning guidance tailored to situations involving chemical, biological, or nuclear/radiological weapons.

Upon arrival at the FBI Command Post or forward location, the DEST may act as a stand alone advisory team to the SAC providing recommended courses of action. While the DEST can operate as an advance element of the JOC, DEST deployment does not have to precede JOC activation. Upon JOC activation, the SAC is the Federal On-Scene Commander (OSC). The Federal OSC serves as the on-scene manager for the United States Government and coordinates the actions of the JOC Command Group. The DEST consequence management component merges into the JOC structure under the leadership of the Senior FEMA Official.

1.   The role of the FBI is to:

   a.   Designate a Federal OSC,

   b.   Deploy the DEST if warranted and approved, and provide liaison to State and local authorities as appropriate,

   c.   Establish multi-agency coordination structures, as appropriate, at the incident scene, area, and national level in order to:

      (1)   Coordinate the determination of operational objectives, strategies, and priorities for the use of critical resources that have been allocated to the situation, and communicate multi-agency decisions back to individual agencies and incidents.

      (2)   Coordinate the evaluation of emerging incidents, priority-zation of incidents, and projection of future needs.

      (3)   Establish a Joint Information Center and coordinate information dissemination.

2.   The role of FEMA is to:

   a.   Activate the appropriate FRP elements, as needed,

   b.   Designate and deploy an individual to serve as the Senior FEMA Official to the JOC. Primary responsibilities include:

      (1)   Managing the Consequence Management Group.

      (2)   Serving as senior consequence management official on the Command Group.

      (3)   Designate an individual to work with the FBI liaison to screen intelligence for consequence management related implications.

    c.   Identify the appropriate agencies to staff the JOC Consequence Management Group and advise the FBI. With FBI concurrence, notify consequence management agencies to request they deploy representatives to the JOC.

C. Response Operations

The response operations phase involves those activities necessary for an actual Federal response to address the immediate and short-term effects of a terrorist threat or incident. These activities support an emergency response with a bilateral focus on the achievement of law enforcement goals and objectives, and the planning and execution of consequence management activities to address the effects of a terrorist incident. Prior to the use or functioning of a WMD, crisis management activities will generally have priority. When an incident results in the use of WMD, consequence management activities will generally have priority. Activities may overlap and/or run concurrently during the emergency response, and are dependent on the threat and/or the strategies for responding to the incident. Events may preclude certain activities from occurring, particularly in an attack without prior warning.

D. Response Deactivation

Each Federal agency will discontinue emergency response operations under the CONPLAN when advised that their assistance is no longer required in support of the FBI, or when their statutory responsibilities have been fulfilled. Upon determination that applicable law enforcement goals and objectives have been met, no further immediate threat exists, and that Federal crisis management actions are no longer required, the Attorney General, in consultation with the FBI Director and the FEMA Director, shall transfer the LFA role to FEMA. The Federal OSC will deactivate and discontinue emergency response operations under the CONPLAN. Prior to this activity, the Federal OSC will apprise the senior officials representing agencies in the JOC Command Group of the intent to deactivate in order to confirm agreement for this decision. Consequence management support to the State and local government(s) impacted by the incident may continue for a very long period. Termination of consequence management assistance will be handled according to the procedures established in the FRP.

E.   Recovery

The State and local governments share primary responsibility for planning the recovery of the affected area. Recovery efforts will be initiated at the request of the State or local governments following mutual agreement of the agencies involved and confirmation from the LFA that the incident has stabilized and that no further threat exists to public health and safety. The Federal government will assist the State and local governments in developing mitigation and recovery plans, with FEMA coordinating the overall activity of the Federal agencies involved in this phase.

APPENDIX A: ACRONYMS

CONPLAN	Concept of Operations Plan
DEST	Domestic Emergency Support Team
DOD	Department of Defense
DOE	Department of Energy
DOJ	Department of Justice
EM	Emergency Management
EMS	Emergency Medical Services
EOC	Emergency Operations Center
EPA	Environmental Protection Agency
ERT	Evidence Response Team (FBI)
FBI	Federal Bureau of Investigation
FCO	Federal Coordinating Officer
FEMA	Federal Emergency Management Agency
FRP	Federal Response Plan
HAZMAT	Hazardous Materials
HHS	Department of Health and Human Services
HMRU	Hazardous Materials Response Unit
JIC	Joint Information Center
JIISE	Joint Interagency Intelligence Support Element
JOC	Joint Operations Center
JTTF	Joint Terrorism Task Force

ICS	Incident Command System
LFA	Lead Federal Agency
NCP	National Oil and Hazardous Substances Pollution Contingency Plan
NOC	Negotiations Operations Center
OSC	On-Scene Commander (FBI) On-Scene Coordinator (EPA)
PIO	Public Information Officer
PDD-39	Presidential Decision Directive 39
ROC	Regional Operations Center
SAC	Special Agent-in-Charge
SFO	Senior FEMA Official
SIOC	Strategic Information and Operations Center
STOC	Sniper Tactical Operations Center
TOC	Tactical Operations Center
UC	Unified Command
USCG	United States Coast Guard
WMD	Weapon of Mass Destruction

APPENDIX B: DEFINITIONS

Assessment - The evaluation and interpretation of measurements and other information to provide a basis for decision-making.

Combating Terrorism - The full range of Federal programs and activities applied against terrorism, domestically and abroad, regardless of the source or motive.

Consequence Management - Consequence management is predominantly an emergency management function and includes measures to protect public health and safety, restore essential government services, and provide emergency relief to governments, businesses, and individuals affected by the consequences of terrorism. In an actual or potential terrorist incident, a consequence management response will be managed by FEMA using structures and resources of the Federal Response Plan (FRP). These efforts will include support missions as described in other Federal operations plans, such as predictive modeling, protective action recommendations, and mass decontamination.

Coordinate - To advance systematically an exchange of information among principals who have or may have a need to know certain information in order to carry out their role in a response.

Counterterrorism - The full range of activities directed against terrorism, including preventive, deterrent, response and crisis management efforts.

Crisis Management - Crisis management is predominantly a law enforcement function and includes measures to identify, acquire, and plan the use of resources needed to anticipate, prevent, and/or resolve a threat or act of terrorism. In a terrorist incident, a crisis management response may include traditional law enforcement missions, such as intelligence, surveillance, tactical operations, negotiations, forensics, and investigations, as well as technical support missions, such as agent identification, search, render safe procedures, transfer and disposal, and limited decontamination. In addition to the traditional law enforcement missions, crisis management also includes assurance of public health and safety.

Disaster Field Office (DFO) - The office established in or near the designated area to support Federal and State response and recovery operations. The Disaster Field Office houses the Federal Coordinating Officer (FCO), the Emergency Response Team, and, where possible, the State Coordinating Officer and support Staff.

Emergency - Any natural or man-caused situation that results in or may result in substantial injury or harm to the population or substantial damage to or loss of property.

Emergency Operations Center (EOC)- The site from which civil government officials (municipal, county, State and Federal) exercise direction and control in an emergency.

Emergency Public Information - Information which is disseminated primarily in anticipation of an emergency or at the actual time of an emergency and in addition to providing information, frequently directs actions, instructs, and transmits direct orders.

Emergency Response Team - (1) A team composed of Federal program and support personnel, which FEMA activates and deploys into an area affected by a major disaster or emergency. This team assists the FCO in carrying out his/her responsibilities under the Stafford Act, the declaration, applicable laws, regulations, and the FEMA-State agreement. (2) The team is an interagency team, consisting of the lead representative from each Federal department or agency assigned primary responsibility for an Emergency support Function and key members of the FCO's staff, formed to assist the FCO in carrying out his/her responsibilities. The team provides a forum for coordinating the overall Federal consequence management response requirements.

Emergency Support Function - A functional area of response activity established to facilitate coordinated Federal delivery of assistance required during the response phase to save lives, protect property and health, and maintain public safety. These functions represent those types of Federal assistance which the State likely will need most because of the overwhelming impact of a catastrophic event on local and State resources.

Evacuation - Organized, phased, and supervised dispersal of civilians from dangerous or potentially dangerous areas, and their reception and care in safe areas.

Federal Coordinating Officer (FCO) - (1) The person appointed by the FEMA Director, or in his/her absence, the FEMA Deputy Director, or alternatively the FEMA Associate Director for Response and Recovery, following a declaration of a major disaster or of an emergency by the President, to coordinate Federal assistance. The FCO initiates action immediately to assure that Federal Assistance is provided in accordance with the declaration, applicable laws, regulations, and the FEMA-State agreement. (2) The FCO is the senior Federal official appointed in accordance with the provisions of Public Law 93-288, as amended (the Stafford Act), to coordinate the overall consequence management response and recovery activities. The FCO represents the President as provided by Section 303 of the Stafford Act for the purpose of coordinating the administration of Federal relief activities in the designated area. Additionally, the FCO is delegated responsibilities and performs those for the FEMA Director as outlined in Executive Order 12148 and those responsibilities delegated to the FEMA Regional Director in the Code of Federal Regulations, Title 44, Part 205.

Federal On-Scene Commander (OSC) - The FBI official designated upon JOC activation to ensure appropriate coordination of the overall United States government response with Federal, State and local authorities, until such time as the Attorney General transfers the LFA role to FEMA.

Federal Response Plan (FRP) - (1) The plan designed to address the consequences of any disaster or emergency situation in which there is a need for Federal assistance under the authorities of the Robert T. Stafford Disaster Relief and Emergency Assistance Act, 42 U.S.C. 5 121 et seq. (2) The FRP is the Federal government's plan of action for assisting affected States and local jurisdictions in the event of a major disaster or emergency.

First Responder - Local police, fire, and emergency medical personnel who first arrive on the scene of an incident and take action to save lives, protect property, and meet basic human needs.

Joint Information Center (JIC) - A center established to coordinate the Federal public information activities on-scene. It is the central point of contact for all news media at the scene of the incident. Public information officials from all participating Federal agencies should collocate at the JIC. Public information officials from participating State and local agencies also may collocate at the JIC.

Joint Interagency Intelligence Support Element (JIISE) - The JIISE is an interagency intelligence component designed to fuse intelligence information from the various agencies participating in a response to a WMD threat or incident within an FBI JOC. The JIISE is an expanded version of the investigative/intelligence component which is part of the standardized FBI command post structure. The JIISE manages five functions including: security, collections management, current intelligence, exploitation, and dissemination.

Joint Operations Center (JOC) - Established by the LFA under the operational control of the Federal OSC, as the focal point for management and direction of onsite activities, coordination/establishment of State requirements/priorities, and coordination of the overall Federal response.

Lead Agency - The Federal department or agency assigned lead responsibility under U.S. law to manage and coordinate the Federal response in a specific functional area. For the purposes of the CONPLAN, there are two lead agencies, the FBI for Crisis Management and FEMA for Consequence Management. Lead agencies support the overall Lead Federal Agency (LFA) during all phases of the response.

Lead Federal Agency (LFA) - The agency designated by the President to lead and coordinate the overall Federal response is referred to as the LFA and is determined by the type of emergency. In general, an LFA establishes operational structures and procedures to assemble and work with agencies providing direct support to the LFA in order to provide an initial assessment of the situation; develop an action plan; monitor and update operational priorities; and ensure each agency exercises its concurrent and distinct authorities under US law and supports the LFA in carrying out the President's relevant policy. Specific responsibilities of an LFA vary according to the agency's unique statutory authorities.

Liaison - An agency official sent to another agency to facilitate interagency communications and coordination.

Local Government - Any county, city, village, town, district, or political subdivision of any State, and Indian tribe or authorized tribal organization, or Alaska Native village or organization, including any rural community or unincorporated town or village or any other public entity.

On-Scene Coordinator (OSC) - The Federal official pre-designated by the EPA and U.S. Coast Guard to coordinate and direct response and removals under the National Oil and Hazardous Substances Pollution Contingency Plan.

Public Information Officer - Official at headquarters or in the field responsible for preparing and coordinating the dissemination of public information in cooperation with other responding Federal, State, and local agencies.

Recovery - Recovery, in this document, includes all types of emergency actions dedicated to the continued protection of the public or to promoting the resumption of normal activities in the affected area.

Recovery Plan - A plan developed by each State, with assistance from the responding Federal agencies, to restore the affected area.

Regional Director - The Director of one of FEMA's ten regional offices and principal representative for working with other Federal regions, State and local governments, and the private sector in that jurisdiction.

Regional Operations Center (ROC) - The temporary operations facility for the coordination of Federal response and recovery activities, located at the FEMA Regional Office (or at the Federal Regional Center) and led by the FEMA Regional Director or Deputy Regional Director until the Disaster Field Office becomes operational.

Response - Those activities and programs designed to address the immediate and short-term effects of the onset of an emergency or disaster.

Senior FEMA Official (SFO) - The official appointed by the Director of FEMA, or his representative, that is responsible for deploying to the JOC to: (1) serve as the senior interagency consequence management representative on the Command Group, and (2) manage and coordinate activities taken by the Consequence Management Group.

State Coordinating Officer - An official designated by the Governor of the affected State, upon a declaration of a major disaster or emergency, to coordinate State and local disaster assistance efforts with those of the Federal government, and to act in cooperation with the FCO to administer disaster recovery efforts.

Terrorism - Terrorism includes the unlawful use of force or violence against persons or property to intimidate or coerce a government, the civilian population, or any segment thereof, in furtherance of political or social objectives.

Weapon of Mass Destruction (WMD) - A WMD is any device, material, or substance used in a manner, in a quantity or type, or under circumstances evidencing an intent to cause death or serious injury to persons or significant damage to property.

Public Health Emergency Response: The CDC Role

Strengthening the nation's public health system to protect Americans during public health emergencies

January 2001

CDC's responsibility, on behalf of the Department of Health and Human Services (DHHS), is to provide national leadership in the public health and medical communities in a concerted effort to detect, diagnose, respond to, and prevent illnesses, including those that could occur as a result of bioterrorism or any other deliberate attempt to harm the health of our citizens. This task is an integral part of CDC's overall mission to monitor and protect the health of the U.S. population.

A strong and flexible public health infrastructure is the best defense against any disease outbreak— naturally or intentionally caused. CDC's on-going initiatives to strengthen disease surveillance and response at the local, state, and federal levels complement efforts to detect and contain diseases caused by the biological agents that might be used as weapons.

Unlike an explosion or a tornado, a bioterrorist attack could be invisible and silent, and thus would be difficult to detect at first. The release of a biological agent or chemical toxin might not have an immediate and visible impact because of the delay between exposure and onset of illness, or incubation period. The initial responders to such a biological attack would include local, county, and city health officers, hospital staff, members of the outpatient medical community, and a wide range of response personnel in the public health system.

CDC and the public health community at large are not involved in assessing the likelihood of a bioterrorism threat. Our responsibility in the overall federal counterterrorism response is to improve the public health community's preparedness to detect illness that may be related to a bioterrorism threat, and develop the appropriate public health structure and contingency plans to respond effectively in the event of a bioterrorism incident.

In recent years, it has become more common for public health disease outbreak investigators to consider the possibility of a terrorist event when they investigate the cause of an outbreak. It is not always clear in the first stages of an epidemiologic investigation whether an outbreak has a natural or man-made cause. The investigative skills, diagnostic techniques, and physical resources required to detect and diagnose a disease outbreak are the same ones required to identify and respond to a silent bioterrorist attack.

CDC has a strategic plan to improve our preparedness for responding to any threat or actual act of bioterrorism. In 1998, CDC issued *Preventing Emerging Infectious Diseases: A Strategy for the 21st Century,* which describes CDC's plan for combating today's emerging diseases and preventing those of tomorrow.

The effort to upgrade public health capabilities locally and nationally to respond to biological and chemical terrorism is underway. CDC, working in collaboration with State and local health departments, many other public health partners, and other Federal agencies, is leading the effort.

Four areas of preparedness are featured in CDC's strategic planning: 1) reinforce systems of public health surveillance to ensure rapid detection of unusual outbreaks; 2) build epidemiologic capacity to investigate and control health threats from such events; 3) enhance public health laboratory capability to diagnose the illness and identify etiologic agents most likely to be used in bioterrorist events; and, 4) develop and coordinate communications systems with other government agencies and the general public to disseminate critical information and allay unnecessary fear.

An improved public health infrastructure that can detect disease outbreaks early and provide treatment and disease control is important not only for issues related to bioterrorism but for all infectious diseases. In the best-case scenario, an observant, well trained health worker would recognize that something out of the ordinary has occurred and alert public health authorities through prearranged channels. For some infectious disease agents, we might have only a short window of opportunity— between the time the first cases are identified and a second wave of people become ill— to determine that an attack has occurred, to identify the organism, and to prevent further spread. Protection against bioterrorism requires a strong public health system at the local, state, and national levels.

Training Disease Detectives

First and foremost, local communities must have a coordinated response plan to a possible bioterrorist attack. These response plans should include law enforcement, medical first responders and public health officials. The FBI has jurisdiction for terrorism response. If bioterrorism is suspected, the local emergency response system should be activated.

CDC's Epidemic Intelligence Service (EIS) trains personnel to respond to outbreaks and other disaster situations to aid state and local officials in the identification of potential causes and implement appropriate solutions. It is interesting to remember that the EIS was established during the Cold War in response to the threat of biological warfare.

In addition, CDC trains Public Health Prevention Service (PHPS) specialists who can provide on-site programmatic support to extend the manpower of state and local public health staff.

Another HHS program, the Metropolitan Medical Response System, also helps communities prepare for coordinated response. So far, 97 cities nationwide have received assistance.

Laboratory Capacity

In the event of a bioterrorist attack, rapid diagnosis will be critical to the immediate implementation of prevention and treatment measures. Future events possibly even could involve organisms that have been genetically engineered to increase their virulence, manifest antibiotic resistance, or evade natural or vaccine-induced immunity.

Because none of the biological agents considered most likely to be used as bio-weapons are currently major public health problems in the United States, we have had limited capacity to diagnose them, either at the state and local or federal level. CDC is working with state health department laboratories to increase the capacity to identify possible disease agents.

We must also prepare for the possible use of other agents as bioterrorist threats.

CDC has helped State health departments acquire the capacity to detect outbreaks of foodborne diseases, including accidental as well as possible deliberate contamination. Providing state health departments with the capacity to detect outbreaks of diseases that could be caused by terrorists can help avert possible widespread consequences.

CDC has met with public health officials of various professional societies and at state and local public health laboratory levels to develop and enhance reference laboratory activity in key geographic areas. CDC awarded cooperative agreements to health departments to help upgrade state and local surveillance capabilities.

As part of the implementation of CDC's plan for emerging infections, CDC has established the Epidemiologic and Laboratory Capacity (ELC) program to help state and large local health departments develop the skills and resources to address whatever unforeseen infectious disease challenges may arise in the twenty-first century. One of the specific aims of the ELC program is the development of innovative systems for early detection and investigation of outbreaks. State and large local health departments will receive continued support from the ELC program.

Early Detection

CDC has helped establish sentinel disease detection systems that involve local networks of clinicians and other health care providers. One such network includes emergency departments at hospitals in large U.S. cities. Another includes travel medicine clinics in the United States, plus overseas. A third network includes over 500 infectious disease specialists throughout the country.

CDC is using these and other provider-based networks to alert and inform the medical community so that health workers can help recognize and assess unusual infectious disease threats.

CDC has also entered into agreements with selected State health departments, in collaboration with local academic, government, and private sector organizations, to establish Emerging Infections Program (EIP) sites that conduct active, population-based surveillance for selected diseases, as well as for unexplained deaths and severe illnesses in previously healthy people.

Epidemiology and Laboratory Capacity cooperative agreement funds have been used to provide more than 75 public health professionals (including 24 epidemiologists and 25 laboratorians) to meet some needs in the health departments.

Rapid Communications and Information Access

One of the major objectives in CDC's emerging infections plan is to improve CDC's ability to communicate with state and local health departments, U.S. quarantine stations, health care professionals, other public health partners, and the public.

In the event of an intentional release of a biological agent, rapid and secure communications will be especially crucial to ensure a prompt and coordinated response. In the case of some infectious diseases, each hour's delay would increase the probability that another group of people will be exposed, and the outbreak could spread both in number and in geographical range.

CDC may also need to communicate with WHO and with the ministries of health of other nations, especially if persons exposed in the United States have traveled to another country. Because of the ease and frequency of modern travel, an outbreak caused by a bioterrorist could quickly become an international problem.

To ensure rapid communication and access to critical health information, CDC is implementing the national Health Alert Network (HAN), in partnership with the National Association of County and City Health Officials (NACCHO), the Association of State and Territorial Health Officials (ASTHO), and other health organizations.

The HAN will establish communications, information, distance-learning, and organizational infrastructure for a new level of defense against bioterrorism and other health threats, linking all public health agencies at the local, state, and Federal levels via 1) continuous, high-speed connection to the Internet, 2) broadcast communications, and 3) satellite- and Web-based distance-learning.

National Pharmaceutical Stockpile (NPSP)

Once the cause of a terrorist-sponsored outbreak was determined, specific drugs, vaccines, and antitoxins might be needed to treat the victims and to prevent further spread.

Depending upon the pathogen that causes the outbreak, appropriate medical supplies may not be readily available to local responders, or in the quantity needed, since these organisms are uncommon causes of disease in the United States.

CDC has developed of a stockpile of pharmaceuticals to be able to reach victims of an incident anywhere in the continental U.S. within 12 hours. This system was proven for the first time when tons of medical supplies reached New York City within seven hours of deployment following the attack on the World Trade Center. CDC is developing an infrastructure for rapid delivery of pharmaceuticals and adequate monitoring and record-keeping systems.

Statement of James M. Hughes, M.D.

Director
National Center for Infectious Diseases
Centers for Disease Control and Prevention
Department of Health and Human Services

Before the Subcommittee on National Security, Veterans Affairs, and International Relations
Committee on Government Reform
U.S. House of Representatives

July 23, 2001

Good afternoon, Mr. Chairman and Members of the Subcommittee. I am Dr. James M. Hughes, Director, National Center for Infectious Diseases (NCID), Centers for Disease Control and Prevention (CDC). I am accompanied by Dr. James W. LeDuc, Acting Director of NCID's Division of Viral and Rickettsial Diseases. Thank you for the invitation to update you on CDC's public health response to the threat of bioterrorism. I will discuss the overall goals of our bioterrorism preparedness program, and I will briefly address specific activities aimed at preparedness for a deliberate release of variola virus, the pathogen responsible for smallpox.

Vulnerability of the Civilian Population

In the past, an attack with a biological agent was considered very unlikely; however, now it seems entirely possible. Many experts believe that it is no longer a matter of "if" but "when" such an attack will occur. Unlike an explosion or a tornado, in a biological event, it is unlikely that a single localized place or cluster of people will be identified for traditional first responder activity. The initial responders to such a biological attack will include emergency department and hospital staff, members of the outpatient medical community, and a wide range of response personnel in the public health system, in conjunction with county and city health officers. Increased vigilance and preparedness for unexplained illnesses and injuries are an essential part of the public health effort to protect the American people against bioterrorism.

Public Health Leadership

The Department of Health and Human Services (DHHS) anti-bioterrorism efforts are focused on improving the nation's public health surveillance network to quickly detect and identify the biological agent that has been released; strengthening the capacities for medical response, especially at the local level; expanding the stockpile of pharmaceuticals for use if needed; expanding research on disease agents that might be released, rapid methods for identifying biological agents, and improved treatments and vaccines; and preventing bioterrorism by regulation of the shipment of hazardous biological agents or toxins. On July 10, 2001, Secretary Thompson named CDC's Dr. Scott Lillibridge as his special advisor to lead the Department's coordinated bioterrorism initiative.

As the Nation's disease prevention and control agency, it is CDC's responsibility on behalf of DHHS to provide national leadership in the public health and medical communities in a concerted effort to detect, diagnose, respond to, and prevent illnesses, including those that occur as a result of a deliberate release of biological agents. This task is an integral part of CDC's overall mission to monitor and protect the health of the U.S. population.

In 1998, CDC issued *Preventing Emerging Infectious Diseases: A Strategy for the 21st Century*, which describes CDC's plan for combating today's emerging diseases and preventing those of tomorrow. It focuses on four goals, each of which has direct relevance to preparedness for bioterrorism: disease surveillance and outbreak response; applied research to develop diagnostic tests, drugs, vaccines, and surveillance tools; infrastructure and training; and disease prevention and control. This plan emphasizes the need to be prepared for the unexpected— whether it is a naturally occurring influenza pandemic or the deliberate release of smallpox by a terrorist. It is within the context of these overall goals that CDC has begun to address preparing our Nation's public health infrastructure to respond to acts of biological terrorism. Copies of this CDC plan have been provided previously to the Subcommittee. In addition, CDC presented in March a report to the Senate entitled "Public Health's Infrastructure: A Status Report." Recommendations in this report complement the strategies outlined for emerging infectious diseases and preparedness and response to bioterrorism. These recommendations include training of the public health workforce, strengthening of data and communications systems, and improving the public health systems at the state and local level.

CDC's Strategic Plan for Bioterrorism

On April 21, 2000, CDC issued a Morbidity and Mortality Weekly Report (MMWR), *Biological and Chemical Terrorism: Strategic Plan for Preparedness and Response - Recommendations of the CDC Strategic Planning Workgroup*, which outlines steps for strengthening public health and healthcare capacity to protect the nation against these threats. This report reinforces the work CDC has been contributing to this effort since 1998 and lays a framework from which to enhance public health infrastructure. In keeping with the message of this report, five key focus areas have been identified which provide the foundation for local, state, and federal planning efforts: Preparedness and Prevention, Detection and Surveillance, Diagnosis and Characterization of Biological and Chemical Agents, Response, and Communication. These areas capture the goals of CDC's Bioterrorism Preparedness and Response Program for general bioterrorism preparedness, as well as the more specific goals targeted towards preparing for the potential intentional reintroduction of smallpox. As was highlighted in the recent *Dark Winter* exercise, smallpox virus is of particular concern.

Preparedness and Prevention

CDC is working to ensure that all levels of the public health community— federal, state, and local— are prepared to work in coordination with the medical and emergency response communities to address the public health consequences of biological and chemical terrorism.

CDC is creating diagnostic and epidemiological performance standards for state and local health departments and will help states conduct drills and exercises to assess local readiness for bioterrorism. In addition, CDC, the National Institutes of Health (NIH), the Department of Defense (DOD), and other agencies are supporting and encouraging research to address scientific issues related to bioterrorism. In some cases, new vaccines, antitoxins, or innovative drug treatments need to be developed or stocked. Moreover, we need to learn more about the pathogenesis and epidemiology of the infectious diseases which do not affect the U.S. population currently. We have only limited knowledge about how artificial methods of dispersion may affect the infection rate, virulence, or impact of these biological agents.

In 1999, the Institute of Medicine released its *Assessment of Future Scientific Needs for Live Variola Virus*, which formed the basis for a phased research agenda to address several scientific issues related to smallpox. This research agenda is a collaboration between CDC, NIH, and DOD and is being undertaken in the high-containment laboratory at CDC with the concurrence of WHO. The research addresses: 1) the use of modern serologic and molecular diagnostic techniques to improve diagnostic capabilities for smallpox, 2) the evaluation of antiviral compounds for activity against the smallpox virus, and 3) further study of the pathogenesis of smallpox by the development of an animal model that mimics human smallpox infection. To date, genetic material from 45 different strains of smallpox virus has been extracted and is being evaluated to determine the genetic diversity of different strains of the virus. The NIH, with CDC and DOD collaborators, has funded a Poxvirus Bioinformatics Resource

Center (www.poxvirus.org) to facilitate the analysis of sequence data to aid the development of rapid and specific diagnostic assays, antiviral medicines and vaccines. A dedicated sequencing and bio-informatics laboratory also is being developed at CDC to help further these efforts. This laboratory will also be used to help characterize other potential bioterrorism pathogens. In addition, a team of collaborating scientists has screened over 270 antiviral compounds for activity against smallpox virus and other related poxviruses and have found several compounds which merit further evaluation in animal models. These compounds were evaluated initially in cell cultures, and 27 promising candidates are being further evaluated for efficacy. The identification of one currently licensed compound with in vitro and in vivo efficacy against the smallpox virus has led to the development of an Investigational New Drug (IND) application by NIH and CDC to the FDA for use of this drug, cidofovir, in an emergency situation for treating persons who are diagnosed with smallpox. Researchers also have been funded by NIH to design new anti-smallpox medicines and to create human monoclonal antibodies to replace the limited supply of vaccinia immune globulin that is needed to treat vaccine complications that arise during immunization campaigns.

The Advisory Committee for Immunization Practices (ACIP) worked with CDC to develop updated guidelines for the use of smallpox vaccine. These guidelines were published in the *MMWR* in June 2001 and serve to educate the medical and public health community regarding the recommended routine and emergency uses and medical aspects of the vaccine as well as, the medical aspects of smallpox itself. Several infection control and worker safety issues were also addressed by the ACIP within the updated guidelines.

While we are pursuing the development of additional smallpox vaccine to improve our readiness to respond to a smallpox outbreak, we are also working to ensure that the stores of vaccine that we have in the United States currently are ready for use, including protocols for emergency release and transportation of the vaccine.

Detection and Surveillance

Because the initial detection of a biological terrorist attack will most likely occur at the local level, it is essential to educate and train members of the medical community— both public and private— who may be the first to examine and treat the victims. It is also necessary to upgrade the surveillance systems of state and local health departments, as well as within healthcare facilities such as hospitals, which will be relied upon to spot unusual patterns of disease occurrence and to identify any additional cases of illness. CDC will provide terrorism-related training to epidemiologists and laboratorians, emergency responders, emergency department personnel and other front-line health-care providers, and health and safety personnel. CDC is working to provide educational materials regarding potential bioterrorism agents to the medical and public health communities on its bioterrorism website at www.bt.cdc.gov. For example, we are preparing a video on smallpox vaccination techniques for public health personnel and healthcare providers who may administer vaccine in an emergency situation. CDC is planning to work with partners such as the Johns Hopkins Center for Civilian Biodefense Studies and the Infectious Diseases Society of America to develop training and educational materials for incorporation into medical and public health graduate and post-graduate curricula. With public health partners, CDC is spearheading the development of the National Electronic Disease Surveillance System, which will facilitate automated, timely electronic capture of data from the healthcare system. CDC has also worked with organizations such as the Council of State and Territorial Epidemiologists to ensure that suspected cases of smallpox are immediately reportable in their jurisdictions and that clear lines of communication are in place.

Diagnosis and Characterization of Biological and Chemical Agents

To ensure that prevention and treatment measures can be implemented quickly in the event of a biological or chemical terrorist attack, rapid diagnosis will be critical. CDC is developing guidelines and quality assurance standards for the safe and secure collection, storage, transport, and processing of biologic and environmental samples. In collaboration with other federal and non-federal partners, CDC is co-sponsoring a series of training exercises for state public health laboratory personnel on requirements for the safe use, containment, and transport of dangerous biological agents and toxins. CDC is also enhancing its efforts to foster the safe design and operation of Biosafety Level 3 laboratories, which are required for handling many highly dangerous pathogens. In addition, CDC is helping to limit access to potential terrorist agents by continuing to administer the Select Agent Rule, *Additional Requirements for Facilities Transferring or Receiving Select Agents* (42 CFR Section 72.6), which regulates shipments of certain hazardous biological organisms and toxins. Furthermore, CDC is developing a Rapid Toxic Screen to detect people's exposure to 150 chemical agents using blood or urine samples.

Response

A decisive and timely response to a biological terrorist event involves a fully documented and well rehearsed plan of detection, epidemiologic investigation, and medical treatment for affected persons, and the initiation of disease prevention measures to minimize illness, injury and death. CDC is addressing this by (1) assisting state and local health agencies in developing their plans for investigating and responding to unusual events and unexplained illnesses and (2) bolstering CDC's capacities within the overall federal bioterrorism response effort. CDC is working to formalize current draft plans for the notification and mobilization of personnel and laboratory resources in response to a bioterrorism emergency, as well as overall strategies for vaccination, and development and implementation of other potential outbreak control measures such as quarantine measures. In addition, CDC is working to develop national standards to ensure that respirators used by first responders to terrorist acts provide adequate protection against weapons of terrorism.

Communication Systems

In the event of an intentional release of a biological agent, rapid and secure communications will be especially crucial to ensure a prompt and coordinated response. Thus, strengthening communication among clinicians, emergency rooms, infection control practitioners, hospitals, pharmaceutical companies, and public health personnel is of paramount importance. To this end, CDC is making a significant investment in building the nation's public health communications infrastructure through the Health Alert Network, a nationwide program designed to ensure communications capacity at all local and state health departments (full Internet connectivity and training), ensure capacity to receive distance learning offerings from CDC and others, and ensure capacity to broadcast and receive health alerts at every level. CDC has also established the *Epidemic Information Exchange (EPI-X)*, a secure, Web-based communications system to enhance bioterrorism preparedness efforts by facilitating the sharing of preliminary information about disease outbreaks and other health events among public health officials across jurisdictions and provide experience in the use of secure communications.

An act of terrorism is likely to cause widespread panic, and on-going communication of accurate and up-to-date information will help calm public fears and limit collateral effects of the attack. To assure the most effective response to an attack, CDC is working closely with other federal agencies, including the Food and Drug Administration, NIH, DOD, Department of Justice (DOJ), and the Federal Emergency Management Agency (FEMA).

The National Pharmaceutical Stockpile

As CDC recently reported to this Subcommittee, another integral component of public health preparedness at CDC has been the development of a National Pharmaceutical Stockpile (NPS), which can be mobilized in response to an episode caused by a biological or chemical agent. The role of the CDC's NPS program is to maintain a national repository of life-saving pharmaceuticals and medical material that can be delivered to the site or sites of a biological or chemical terrorism event in order to reduce morbidity and mortality in a civilian population. The NPS is a backup and means of support to state and local first responders, healthcare providers, and public health officials. The NPS program consists of a two-tier response: (1) 12-hour push packages, which are preassembled arrays of pharmaceuticals and medical supplies that can be delivered to the scene of a terrorism event within 12 hours of the federal decision to deploy the assets and that will make possible the treatment or prophylaxis of disease caused by a variety of threat agents; and (2) a Vendor-Managed Inventory (VMI) that can be tailored to a specific threat agent. Components of the VMI will arrive at the scene 24 to 36 hours after activation. CDC has developed this program in collaboration with federal and private sector partners and with input from the states.

Challenges Highlighted in *Dark Winter* Exercise

The CDC has been addressing issues of detection, epidemiologic investigation, diagnostics, and enhanced infrastructure and communications as part of its overall bioterrorism preparedness strategies. The issues that emerged from the recent *Dark Winter* exercise reflected similar themes that need to be addressed.

- *The importance of rapid diagnosis*--Rapid and accurate diagnosis of biological agents will require strong linkages between clinical and public health laboratories. In addition, diagnostic specimens will need to be delivered promptly to CDC, where laboratorians will provide diagnostic confirmatory and reference support.

- *The importance of working through the governors' offices as part of our planning and response efforts*--During the exercise this was demonstrated by Governor Keating. During state-wide emergencies the federal government will need to work with a partner in the state who can galvanize the multiple response communities and government sectors that will be needed, such as the National Guard, the state health department, and the state law enforcement communities. These in turn will need to coordinate with their local counterparts. CDC is refining its planning efforts through grants, policy forums such as the National Governors Association and the National Emergency Management Association, and training activities. CDC also participates with partners such as DOJ and FEMA in planning and implementing national drills such as the recent TOPOFF exercise.

- *Better targeting of limited smallpox vaccine stocks to ensure strategic use of vaccine in persons at highest risk of infection*--It was clear that pre-existing guidance regarding strategic use would have been beneficial and would have accelerated the response at *Dark Winter*. As I mentioned earlier, CDC is working on this issue and is developing guidance for vaccination programs and planning activities.

- *Federal control of the smallpox vaccine at the inception of a national crisis*--Currently, the smallpox vaccine is held by the manufacturer. CDC has worked with the U.S. Marshals Service to conduct an initial security assessment related to a future emergency deployment of vaccine to states. CDC is currently addressing the results of this assessment, along with other issues related to security, movement, and initial distribution of smallpox vaccine.

- The importance of early technical information on the progress of such an epidemic for consideration by decision makers--In *Dark Winter*, this required the implementation of various steps at the local, state, and federal levels to control the spread of disease. This is a complex endeavor and may involve measures ranging from directly observed therapy to quarantine, along with consideration as to who would enforce such measures. Because wide-scale federal quarantine measures have not been implemented in the United States in over 50 years, operational protocols to implement a quarantine of significant scope are needed. CDC hosted a forum on state emergency public health legal authorities to encourage state and local public health officers and their attorneys to examine what legal authorities would be needed in a bioterrorism event. In addition, CDC is reviewing foreign and interstate quarantine regulations to update them in light of modern infectious disease and bioterrorism concerns. CDC will continue this preparation to ensure that such measures will be implemented early in the response to an event.

- *Maintaining effective communications with the media and press during such an emergency*--The need for accurate and timely information during a crisis is paramount to maintaining the trust of the community. Those responsible for leadership in such emergencies will need to enhance their capabilities to deal with the media and get their message to the public. It was clear from *Dark Winter* that large-scale epidemics will generate intense media interest and information needs. CDC has refined its media plan and expanded its communications staff. These personnel will continue to be intimately involved in our planning and response efforts to epidemics.

- *Expanded local clinical services for victims*--DHHS's Office of Emergency Preparedness is working with the other members of the National Disaster Medical System to expand and refine the delivery of medical services for epidemic stricken populations.

CDC will continue to work with partners to address challenges in public health preparedness, such as those raised at *Dark Winter*. For example, work done by CDC staff to model the effects of control measures such as quarantine and vaccination in a smallpox outbreak have highlighted the importance of both public health measures in controlling such an outbreak. The importance of both quarantine and vaccination as outbreak control measures is also supported by historical experience with smallpox epidemics during the eradication era. These issues, as well as overall preparedness planning at the federal level, are currently being addressed and require additional action to ensure that the nation is fully prepared to respond to all acts of biological terrorism, including those involving smallpox.

Conclusion

In conclusion, CDC has made substantial progress to date in enhancing the nation's capability to prepare for and, if need be, respond to a bioterrorist event. The best public health strategy to protect the health of civilians against biological terrorism is the development, organization, and enhancement of public health prevention systems and tools. Priorities include strengthened public health laboratory capacity, increased surveillance and outbreak investigation capacity, and health communications, education, and training at the federal, state, and local levels. Not only will this approach ensure that we are prepared for deliberate bioterrorist threats, but it will also ensure that we will be able to recognize and control naturally occurring new or re-emerging infectious diseases. A strong and flexible public health infrastructure is the best defense against any disease outbreak.

Terrorist Threats Against America

Ambassador Francis X. Taylor, Coordinator for
Counterterrorism

**Testimony to the Committee on International Relations
Washington, DC
September 25, 2001**

Mr. Chairman and Members of the Committee:

I appreciate the opportunity to meet with you and discuss the terrorist threats facing the United States and the world. We need to work together in the task of confronting the heightened terrorist challenge and deterring terrorists and their supporters in the future.

Your Committee's support for our programs in the fight against terrorism has been very helpful in the past and I look forward to working closely with you as we begin our campaign to rid the world of the terrorist menace that threatens all the world's nations. With your permission, I have a more detailed statement to submit for the record. My remarks will highlight my statement for the record.

Before we begin, I want to express my condolence to the families of the thousands of Americans and citizens from more than 80 other nations who were killed, injured, or terrorized by these horrific acts against humanity. I also want to thank the thousands of police officers, firefighters, emergency service and medical personnel and many others who responded so magnificently and have worked tirelessly to save lives and avert greater tragedy. Their efforts in these extraordinary circumstances demonstrate the indomitable American spirit. We are proud of them all and what they represent.

The events in New York and Washington on September 11, 2001 were not just an attack on America and Americans. The World Trade Center bombing claimed victims from some 80 nations— from our close neighbors Canada and Mexico to countries as far away as Australia and Zimbabwe, and large numbers from Britain, India, and Pakistan. For many countries, including ours, this attack claimed the lives of the largest numbers of their citizens in a terrorist incident. These terrorist attacks may have been conceived as a blow against America but in reality they were attacks against all civilized people.

There is no excuse, no justification, no rationalization for these acts of mass murder against innocent people. Those who try to excuse, condone and support groups involved in this activity are no better than the terrorists as their support encourages even more horrific acts like these. Our campaign will go after terrorist groups and their supporters and eliminate them as a threat to civilization.

President Bush said bluntly in his address to Congress last Thursday:

"Every nation, in every region, now has a decision to make. Either you are with us, or you are with the terrorists."

This Administration is mobilizing an international coalition against the terrorists and those who support them. From around the world, countries have come forward, both individually and through their multilateral associations, to condemn these acts and to offer support for our campaign. While the ability of countries to contribute may vary, each recognizes that the attack against the World Trade Center is an attack against all nations, and future attacks must be deterred.

Trends

Mr. Chairman, a brief understanding of history and context are important in mobilizing for this effort. In your letter of invitation to testify today, you asked me to comment on what this new terrorist trend means. To summarize, in some ways the September 11 attacks do not reflect a brand new trend as much as a quantitative increase in the terrorists' sophistication, planning and willingness to cause large scale destruction and loss of life. During much of the 1970's, most of the terrorism directed against the U.S. and our allies was supported and funded by State sponsors— such as Libya, Syria, Iran and Iraq.

In the early 1990's, we saw the emergence of radical fundamentalist terrorist groups that relied not on state sponsors but primarily on funds raised independently through front companies and so-called charitable contributions. Unlike their predecessors of the 70's and 80's, these groups were distinguished by the fact that they were loosely knit international networks. Some had ties stemming from their involvement in the successful effort by the Afghan people to throw out the occupying forces of the former Soviet Union. It was from this group that Islamic extremist "Afghan Alumni" formed the group al-Qaida, which means "The Base" in Arabic. Al-Qaida is essentially a holding company comprised of many terrorist groups and independent cells. The President and CEO of this holding company is Usama Bin Laden, the 17th son of a wealthy Saudi businessman and veteran of the war in Afghanistan.

Bin Ladin's goal is to remove the American presence from Saudi Arabia and other Islamic Nations and to create an Islamic utopia in what is now the Islamic world. He sees the United States as the major impediment to his goal and has vowed to attack America and Americans to undermine our influence on the world stage.

While some attacks associated with al-Qaida were aimed against specific U.S. military targets, such as USS Cole in Yemen, others were aimed at civilians, such as the bombing of the World Trade Center in 1993 and the 1998 bombings of the U.S. embassies in Tanzania and Kenya that killed over 200 Africans, as well as 12 Americans. Other major plots to kill large numbers of people were foiled, such as an attempt at the end of 1999 to attack a hotel and a Christian religious site in Jordan, a plot to blow up civilian airliners in the Philippines, and a plan to attack Los Angeles airport.

One result of the terrorists' stark "us" vs. "them" attitude is their willingness to kill large numbers of innocent people in suicide attacks without claiming responsibility or stating a measurable demand. In the past, when terrorists hijacked aircraft or took over a building, they did so in pursuit of specific and quantifiable political goals, such as forcing governments to release previously captured colleagues or the media to publish manifestos. The September 11 attacks were a continuation of the trend to inflict maximum casualties, without regard to loss of life or likelihood of achieving specific demands. The planners used a ghastly scenario of the kind that could be imagined only by people so full of hatred that they are beyond the civilized pale.

Challenges

The challenges in meeting this threat are immense. The September 11 terrorists apparently had enough money to make their preparations many months if not years in advance. They developed a network of cells; it will be a real effort to root out those that remain. These groups and perhaps others do not operate in a traditional top-down structure but are loosely knit. We will meet the challenges.

As President Bush told Congress last Thursday night, "We will direct every resource at our command— every means of diplomacy, every tool of intelligence, every instrument of law enforcement, every financial influence, and every necessary weapon of war— to the disruption and to the defeat of the global terror network."

Our efforts include encouraging the gathering and increased sharing of good intelligence, rooting out terrorist cells, identifying and disrupting terrorist money flows, and assisting countries to tighten their border security, law enforcement, and intelligence capability.

The global coalition I mentioned earlier in my testimony is a key element. We are urging other countries to work with us. We are willing to exert diplomatic and economic pressures against countries that do not cooperate in counterterrorism efforts. International cooperation is essential at all levels and for the long term.

Last week I traveled with Deputy Secretary Armitage and several other colleagues to meet with our Russian counterparts. The trip during these busy times underscores the importance of our efforts to cooperate with countries with which we have a mutual interest.

Terrorist Funding

There are a number of areas in which we are seeking international cooperation; I would like to highlight one in particular.

We are encouraging other countries to join in our efforts to clamp down on terrorist fund raising and money transfers. Funding is a critical element in these large-scale terrorist operations and in the recruiting of supporters. We need to choke it off.

The Executive Order signed by the President yesterday is part of that effort.

Another important tool in countering terrorism fundraising is the Antiterrorism and Effective Death Penalty Act (AEDPA) of 1996, which you helped steer through Congress as Chairman of the House Judiciary Committee. For the benefit of those not familiar with the legislation, it makes it a criminal offense for persons subject to U.S. jurisdiction to knowingly contribute funds or other material support to groups that the Secretary of State has designated as Foreign Terrorist Organizations. U.S. law also allows freezing of the designated group's assets and denial of visas for members as well as leaders of terrorist organizations. Currently, 31 groups are designated, including al-Qaida.

Mr. Chairman, an important section in the AEDPA is worth repeating for the world at large. I refer to the finding in section 301:

"[F]oreign terrorist organizations that engage in terrorist activity are so tainted by their criminal conduct that any contribution to such an organization facilitates that conduct."

This is a key point. Before they make a contribution to groups supporting terrorists, people around the world need to understand that by doing so they are assisting criminal conduct.

Using this and other legislation as a potential model, we have encouraged and will continue to encourage other countries to tighten up their own laws and regulations in order to curb terrorist fund raising and money transfers. Britain already has done so, and other countries, such as Greece, have new counterterrorism laws or proposed legislation in various stages of consideration. We have met with officials of some of these countries to discuss AEDPA and other laws, and to exchange ideas and suggestions.

In particular, we are working with our G-8 partners to encourage international cooperation in countering money flows to terrorists. The State Department already developed a training course in our Anti-terrorism Training Assistance program to help other countries improve their ability to identify and curb terrorist fund raising and transfers. We encourage other countries with expertise to make similar efforts.

In addition, the Administration is making ratification of the International Convention for the Suppression of the Financing of Terrorism a top priority. The Administration is now finalizing proposed implementing legislation for this Convention, and we strongly encourage the Senate to act swiftly and provide advice and consent to ratification to this treaty.

The Administration last week began discussing with Congress a major counterterrorism bill, the "Anti-terrorism Act of 2001." Although most of the public attention has centered on criminal code provisions that the Justice Department put forward, the State Department also offered contributions for the combined bill. Preliminary discussions already started at the staff level and we would be glad to work with the Committee on provisions of mutual interest.

Programs

Mr. Chairman, there are a number of tools that we have been using to counter terrorism, and we are sharpening and improving them in this new struggle.

Some of the basic elements are not new. Just as old-fashioned, painstaking work is important in fighting ordinary crimes, so fighting terrorism requires a number of unglamorous but proven measures.

On the program front, we are utilizing training-related programs to help combat terrorism overseas and thus also help protect Americans living and travelling abroad. The State Department's Anti-terrorism Training Assistance (ATA) program in which we train foreign security and law enforcement officials is a pillar of this effort. The program provides not only training but also helps promote our policies and improve our contacts with foreign officials to achieve our counterterrorism goals.

Even before the September 11 attacks, we were providing policy and working level seminars and training to assist countries in preparing for or responding to weapons of mass destruction terrorism. We also have developed a Terrorist Interdiction Program (TIP) which utilizes sophisticated computer data base systems and improved communications to help identify potential terrorists who try to cross international borders.

The Department's contribution to the interagency counterterrorism research and development program, the Technical Support Working Group, also helps advance in explosives detection and other areas and bolster our cooperative R&D efforts with Britain, Canada and Israel.

We have proposed increasing our terrorism information reward program, including authority to offer larger rewards. The current maximum reward is $5 million. We propose allowing the Secretary to authorize payment of a higher reward if he determines that doing so would be important to the national interests of the United States.

The international coalition and our bilateral programs I mentioned are just some of the measures we are taking to meet this new challenge. Our response to the horrific events of September 11 will be broad-based and will not be completed in a short time. We are committed to a long term strategic campaign, in concert with the Nations of the World that abhor terrorism, to root out and bring to justice those that use terrorism. We are in for a long haul. As President Bush told the world last week, this will be a lengthy campaign. There are no easy or quick fixes in fighting this danger posed by international terrorism. We must be persistent, and determined. And we will.

With the dedication of the American people, your help and that of our allies overseas, we will succeed. Thank you, Mr. Chairman. I would be happy to take any questions.

Executive Order Establishing Office of Homeland Security and the Homeland Security Council

For Immediate Release
Office of the Press Secretary
October 8, 2001

By the authority vested in me as President by the Constitution and the laws of the United States of America, it is hereby ordered as follows:

Section 1. Establishment. I hereby establish within the Executive Office of the President an Office of Homeland Security (the "Office") to be headed by the Assistant to the President for Homeland Security.

Sec. 2. Mission. The mission of the Office shall be to develop and coordinate the implementation of a comprehensive national strategy to secure the United States from terrorist threats or attacks. The Office shall perform the functions necessary to carry out this mission, including the functions specified in section 3 of this order.

Sec. 3. Functions. The functions of the Office shall be to coordinate the executive branch's efforts to detect, prepare for, prevent, protect against, respond to, and recover from terrorist attacks within the United States.

(a)   National Strategy. The Office shall work with executive departments and agencies, State and local governments, and private entities to ensure the adequacy of the national strategy for detecting, preparing for, preventing, protecting against, responding to, and recovering from terrorist threats or attacks within the United States and shall periodically review and coordinate revisions to that strategy as necessary.

(b)   Detection. The Office shall identify priorities and coordinate efforts for collection and analysis of information within the United States regarding threats of terrorism against the United States and activities of terrorists or terrorist groups within the United States. The Office also shall identify, in coordination with the Assistant to the President for National Security Affairs, priorities for collection of intelligence outside the United States regarding threats of terrorism within the United States.

(i) In performing these functions, the Office shall work with Federal, State, and local agencies, as appropriate, to:

    (A) facilitate collection from State and local governments and private entities of information pertaining to terrorist threats or activities within the United States;

    (B) coordinate and prioritize the requirements for foreign intelligence relating to terrorism within the United

    (C) capabilities and resources to collect intelligence and data relating to terrorist activities or possible terrorist acts within the United States, working with the Assistant to the President for National Security Affairs, as appropriate;

    (D) coordinate development of monitoring protocols and equipment for use in detecting the release of biological, chemical, and radiological hazards; and

    (E) ensure that, to the extent permitted by law, all appropriate and necessary intelligence and law enforcement information relating to homeland security is disseminated to and exchanged among appropriate executive departments and agencies responsible for homeland security and, where appropriate for reasons of homeland security, promote exchange of such information with and among State and local governments and private entities.

(ii) Executive departments and agencies shall, to the extent permitted by law, make available to the Office all information relating to terrorist threats and activities within the United States.

(c) Preparedness. The Office of Homeland Security shall coordinate national efforts to prepare for and mitigate the consequences of terrorist threats or attacks within the United States. In performing this function, the Office shall work with Federal, State, and local agencies, and private entities, as appropriate, to:

(i) review and assess the adequacy of the portions of all Federal emergency response plans that pertain to terrorist threats or attacks within the United States;

(ii) coordinate domestic exercises and simulations designed to assess and practice systems that would be called upon to respond to a terrorist threat or attack within the United States and coordinate programs and activities for training Federal, State, and local employees who would be called upon to respond to such a threat or attack;

(iii) coordinate national efforts to ensure public health preparedness for a terrorist attack, including reviewing vaccination policies and reviewing the adequacy of and, if necessary, increasing vaccine and pharmaceutical stockpiles and hospital capacity;

(iv) coordinate Federal assistance to State and local authorities and nongovernmental organizations to prepare for and respond to terrorist threats or attacks within the United States;

(v) ensure that national preparedness programs and activities for terrorist threats or attacks are developed and are regularly evaluated under appropriate standards and that resources are allocated to improving and sustaining preparedness based on such evaluations; and

(vi) ensure the readiness and coordinated deployment of Federal response teams to respond to terrorist threats or attacks, working with the Assistant to the President for National Security Affairs, when appropriate.

(d) Prevention. The Office shall coordinate efforts to prevent terrorist attacks within the United States. In performing this function, the Office shall work with Federal, State, and local agencies, and private entities, as appropriate, to:

(i) facilitate the exchange of information among such agencies relating to immigration and visa matters and shipments of cargo; and, working with the Assistant to the President for National Security Affairs, ensure coordination among such agencies to prevent the entry of terrorists and terrorist materials and supplies into the United States and facilitate removal of such terrorists from the United States, when appropriate;

(ii) coordinate efforts to investigate terrorist threats and attacks within the United States; and

(iii) coordinate efforts to improve the security of United States borders, territorial waters, and airspace in order to prevent acts of terrorism within the United States, working with the Assistant to the President for National Security Affairs, when appropriate.

(e) Protection. The Office shall coordinate efforts to protect the United States and its critical infrastructure from the consequences of terrorist attacks. In performing this function, the Office shall work with Federal, State, and local agencies, and private entities, as appropriate, to:

(i) strengthen measures for protecting energy production, transmission, and distribution services and critical facilities; other utilities; telecommunications; facilities that produce, use, store, or dispose of nuclear material; and other critical infrastructure services and critical facilities within the United States from terrorist attack;

(ii) coordinate efforts to protect critical public and privately owned information systems within the United States from terrorist attack;

(iii) develop criteria for reviewing whether appropriate security measures are in place at major public and privately owned facilities within the United States;

(iv) coordinate domestic efforts to ensure that special events determined by appropriate senior officials to have national significance are protected from terrorist attack;

(v) coordinate efforts to protect transportation systems within the United States, including railways, highways, shipping, ports and waterways, and airports and civilian aircraft, from terrorist attack;

(vi) coordinate efforts to protect United States livestock, agriculture, and systems for the provision of water and food for human use and consumption from terrorist attack; and

(vii) coordinate efforts to prevent unauthorized access to, development of, and unlawful importation into the United States of, chemical, biological, radiological, nuclear, explosive, or other related materials that have the potential to be used in terrorist attacks.

(f) Response and Recovery. The Office shall coordinate efforts to respond to and promote recovery from terrorist threats or attacks within the United States. In performing this function, the Office shall work with Federal, State, and local agencies, and private entities, as appropriate, to:

(i) coordinate efforts to ensure rapid restoration of transportation systems, energy production, transmission, and distribution systems; telecommunications; other utilities; and other critical infrastructure facilities after disruption by a terrorist threat or attack;

(ii) coordinate efforts to ensure rapid restoration of public and private critical information systems after disruption of a terrorist threat or attack;

(iii) work with the National Economic Council to coordinate efforts to stabilize United States financial markets after a terrorist threat or attack and manage the immediate economic and financial consequences of the incident;

(iv)   coordinate Federal plans and programs to provide medical, financial, and other assistance to victims of terrorist attacks and their families; and

(v)   coordinate containment and removal of biological, chemical, radiological, explosive, or other hazardous materials in the event of a terrorist threat or attack involving such hazards and coordinate efforts to mitigate the effects of such an attack.

(g)   Incident Management. The Assistant to the President for Homeland Security shall be the individual primarily responsible for coordinating the domestic response efforts of all departments and agencies in the event of an imminent terrorist threat and during and in the immediate aftermath of a terrorist attack within the United States and shall be the principal point of contact for and to the President with respect to coordination of such efforts. The Assistant to the President for Homeland Security shall coordinate with the Assistant to the President for National Security Affairs, as appropriate.

(h)   Continuity of Government. The Assistant to the President for Homeland Security, in coordination with the Assistant to the President for National Security Affairs, shall review plans and preparations for ensuring the continuity of the Federal Government in the event of a terrorist attack that threatens the safety and security of the United States Government or its leadership.

(i)   Public Affairs. The Office, subject to the direction of the White House Office of Communications, shall coordinate the strategy of the executive branch for communicating with the public in the event of a terrorist threat or attack within the United States. The Office also shall coordinate the development of programs for educating the public about the nature of terrorist threats and appropriate precautions and responses.

(j)   Cooperation with State and Local Governments and Private Entities. The Office shall encourage and invite the participation of State and local governments and private entities, as appropriate, in carrying out the Office's functions.

(k)   Review of Legal Authorities and Development of Legislative Proposals. The Office shall coordinate a periodic review and assessment of the legal authorities available to executive departments and agencies to permit them to perform the functions described in this order. When the Office determines that such legal authorities are inadequate, the Office shall develop, in consultation with executive departments and agencies, proposals for presidential action and legislative proposals for submission to the Office of Management and Budget to enhance the ability of executive departments and agencies to perform those functions. The Office shall work with State and local governments in assessing the adequacy of their legal authorities to permit them to detect, prepare for, prevent, protect against, and recover from terrorist threats and attacks.

(l) Budget Review. The Assistant to the President for Homeland Security, in consultation with the Director of the Office of Management and Budget (the "Director") and the heads of executive departments and agencies, shall identify programs that contribute to the Administration's strategy for homeland security and, in the development of the President's annual budget submission, shall review and provide advice to the heads of departments and agencies for such programs. The Assistant to the President for Homeland Security shall provide advice to the Director on the level and use of funding in departments and agencies for homeland security-related activities and, prior to the Director's forwarding of the proposed annual budget submission to the President for transmittal to the Congress, shall certify to the Director the funding levels that the Assistant to the President for Homeland Security believes are necessary and appropriate for the homeland security-related activities of the executive branch.

Sec. 4. Administration.

(a) The Office of Homeland Security shall be directed by the Assistant to the President for Homeland Security.

(b) The Office of Administration within the Executive Office of the President shall provide the Office of Homeland Security with such personnel, funding, and administrative support, to the extent permitted by law and subject to the availability of appropriations, as directed by the Chief of Staff to carry out the provisions of this order.

(c) Heads of executive departments and agencies are authorized, to the extent permitted by law, to detail or assign personnel of such departments and agencies to the Office of Homeland Security upon request of the Assistant to the President for Homeland Security, subject to the approval of the Chief of Staff.

Sec. 5. Establishment of Homeland Security Council.

(a) I hereby establish a Homeland Security Council (the "Council"), which shall be responsible for advising and assisting the President with respect to all aspects of homeland security. The Council shall serve as the mechanism for ensuring coordination of homeland security-related activities of executive departments and agencies and effective development and implementation of homeland security policies.

(b)   The Council shall have as its members the President, the Vice President, the Secretary of the Treasury, the Secretary of Defense, the Attorney General, the Secretary of Health and Human Services, the Secretary of Transportation, the Director of the Federal Emergency Management Agency, the Director of the Federal Bureau of Investigation, the Director of Central Intelligence, the Assistant to the President for Homeland Security, and such other officers of the executive branch as the President may from time to time designate. The Chief of Staff, the Chief of Staff to the Vice President, the Assistant to the President for National Security Affairs, the Counsel to the President, and the Director of the Office of Management and Budget also are invited to attend any Council meeting. The Secretary of State, the Secretary of Agriculture, the Secretary of the Interior, the Secretary of Energy, the Secretary of Labor, the Secretary of Commerce, the Secretary of Veterans Affairs, the Administrator of the Environmental Protection Agency, the Assistant to the President for Economic Policy, and the Assistant to the President for Domestic Policy shall be invited to attend meetings pertaining to their responsibilities. The heads of other executive departments and agencies and other senior officials shall be invited to attend Council meetings when appropriate.

(c)   The Council shall meet at the President's direction. When the President is absent from a meeting of the Council, at the President's direction the Vice President may preside. The Assistant to the President for Homeland Security shall be responsible, at the President's direction, for determining the agenda, ensuring that necessary papers are prepared, and recording Council actions and Presidential decisions.

Sec. 6. Original Classification Authority. I hereby delegate the authority to classify information originally as Top Secret, in accordance with Executive Order 12958 or any successor Executive Order, to the Assistant to the President for Homeland Security.

Sec. 7. Continuing Authorities. This order does not alter the existing authorities of United States Government departments and agencies. All executive departments and agencies are directed to assist the Council and the Assistant to the President for Homeland Security in carrying out the purposes of this order.

Sec. 8. General Provisions.

(a)   This order does not create any right or benefit, substantive or procedural, enforceable at law or equity by a party against the United States, its departments, agencies or instrumentalities, its officers or employees, or any other person.

(b)   References in this order to State and local governments shall be construed to include tribal governments and United States territories and other possessions.

(c)   References to the "United States" shall be construed to include United States territories and possessions.

Sec. 9. Amendments to Executive Order 12656. Executive Order 12656 of November 18, 1988, as amended, is hereby further amended as follows:

(a)   Section 101(a) is amended by adding at the end of the fourth sentence: ", except that the Homeland Security Council shall be responsible for administering such policy with respect to terrorist threats and attacks within the United States."

(b)   Section 104(a) is amended by adding at the end: ", except that the Homeland Security Council is the principal forum for consideration of policy relating to terrorist threats and attacks within the United States."

(c)   Section 104(b) is amended by inserting the words "and the Homeland Security Council" after the words "National Security Council."

(d)   The first sentence of section 104(c) is amended by inserting the words "and the Homeland Security Council" after the words "National Security Council."

(e)   The second sentence of section 104(c) is replaced with the following two sentences: "Pursuant to such procedures for the organization and management of the National Security Council and Homeland Security Council processes as the President may establish, the Director of the Federal Emergency Management Agency also shall assist in the implementation of and management of those processes as the President may establish. The Director of the Federal Emergency Management Agency also shall assist in the implementation of national security emergency preparedness policy by coordinating with the other Federal departments and agencies and with State and local governments, and by providing periodic reports to the National Security Council and the Homeland Security Council on implementation of national security emergency preparedness policy."

(f)   Section 201(7) is amended by inserting the words "and the Homeland Security Council" after the words "National Security Council."

(g)   Section 206 is amended by inserting the words "and the Homeland Security Council" after the words "National Security Council."

(h) Section 208 is amended by inserting the words "or the Homeland Security Council" after the words "National Security Council."

George W. Bush
The White House
October 8, 2001